THE ROAD TO CONFIDENCE

THE ROAD
TO CONFIDENCE

by

Dr. Stuart E. Rosenberg

Be strong, and let thy heart take courage.

Psalm 27

JULIAN MESSNER, INC.

NEW YORK

TO HADASSA

A woman of valour who can find?
For her price is far above rubies!

Proverbs xxxi: 10

THE ROAD TO CONFIDENCE

PART I MAKE YOUR START NOW

PART II BE A CONFIDENT PERSON

PART III BEGIN WITH YOURSELF

PART IV   HAVE CONFIDENCE IN OTHERS

A.   UNDERSTAND CONFIDENCE

B.   PREPARE YOURSELF

C. WORK WITH OTHERS

PART V   GUIDE YOUR FAMILY TO A CONFIDENT LIFE

PART VI   KNOW THE WONDER OF CONFIDENCE IN GOD

MAKE
YOUR START
NOW

DETERMINE YOUR OWN LIFE

A schoolboy was in great distress every morning, having forgotten where he put his clothes and books before he went to bed. One evening he devised a plan which he thought would solve his problem. He took a piece of paper and wrote:

"The suit is on the chair, the hat is in the closet. The books are on the desk; the shoes are under the chair. And I am in bed."

Next morning he began to collect his things. They were all in their places. When he came to the last item, he went to look for himself in bed—but his search was in vain.

"Where am I?"—the bewildered cry he let fly is the question so many of us feel deeply. Perhaps we don't know where we are because we don't know who or what we are.

A man is what he thinks he is. He has it in his power to be but a little lower than the angels, or not much higher than the beasts. He has the power of faith or the drive for disloyalty. He can aspire or he can scoff. He can love, but he is also capable of cruel, beastly hate.

But what man feels he is, shapes his behaviour. What we think of ourselves determines what we make of ourselves.

It is reported that an astronomer and a philosopher engaged in an earnest discussion. Said the astronomer:

"Astronomically speaking, what is man? He's but an unimportant speck in a far-flung universe of staggering proportions and tremendous distances."

To which the philosopher answered:

"Astronomically speaking, man is the astronomer! It is in his mind that the distances have meaning. It is man who unlocks the atom and wrests out of it the secret forces that lie within it. Only man can harness these forces. But how he shall harness them—for good or evil—is up to him."

We come back again full circle. What man considers he is, determines what he will do to himself. If man is only a plaything, a tool, a fleeting whimsy of circumstances—then nothing matters. He must live for the moment—pushing, shoving, exploiting. Doomsday is at hand and all striving won't be worth a farthing!

But if he holds on to a religious definition of life, he won't become the beast he easily can be. He will see the crystal springs, not just the muddy waters. He will hear the sweet music about him, not only the rasping grunts and shrieking shouts of man-eating men.

And while he won't shut his eyes or ears to what is evil, he will be inspired to uproot what is bad and wrong. But only when he has a vision of what is good and right. It is the vision of the divine that makes us more truly human. God made man in His own image. And man becomes more human only when he acts as if he understood this.

Who are we? What are we? We are—each of us, every last one of us—children of God. And we must never forget that, not for one moment. For if we do, that's about all the time history will give us.

To live today we need to feel eternity in our hearts.

DON'T WASTE TIME
ON THINGS BEYOND YOUR CONTROL

"Real peace with Russia?" asked one man.

"That would be a wonderful thing," he continued, "but my life is scarred with fear and anxiety. What significance would even this good thing have for me?"

There is a truth here that needs re-stating. The great hopes that come from our social and political opportunities can have little meaning to those who have lost their own hope. To those whose hearts are burdened by unnecessary sorrow, a new atomic reactor has little meaning. The man who is tormented by worry is looking for a different kind of help than that of the Salk vaccine. A troubled heart cannot even see the glory of each day's sunshine.

We are making great technical and social progress, expanding life's horizons. But more than anything else, we must first learn how to live with ourselves. Instead of searching for more physical comforts, some of us might well be advertising: "Wanted: a philosophy of life that will help me keep my integrity and face heroically whatever life has in store for me!"

There is one ingredient necessary for such a philosophy. We need the faith that teaches us how to surrender to the things we cannot control. We have got to learn that we are not gods, and despite our advanced scientific knowledge, we just cannot control all life. We are always subject to the law of God in nature, and so we had better learn how to accept the things we cannot change.

But never resign yourself in despair. Hold on to an unconquerable hope that what you believe is not defeated and what you stand for is not lost.   We may be defeated by death, or by disease, or by a hundred natural causes over which we have no personal control.   But when your hopes and dreams are part of the larger hopes of humanity and not centred only on yourself, you can pick up the broken pieces of life and live on, courageously and confidently.

When a scientist dies, his colleagues mourn him.   They miss his counsel and wisdom, but they do not give up science because of it.   They still hold firm to their life-commitments. When our private world seems shattered, when all goes black and dark, think what your sympathy for the suffering of others can mean to you and to them.   It insures your faith against loss from death or destruction.

It is no good to cry over the children who were never born, for those who passed away, for the fame that was never won, or the riches that have been lost.   When life means more than "me and mine", there is always a lot left to live for.

A shipwrecked refugee on an isolated island trudged for two terrible days and nights carrying his sick young son—the last of the family.   At the second nightfall the child died.   As he buried his beloved, he turned heavenward and said:

"O, Lord, You have taken everything from me—my wife, my home, my worldly possessions, and this, my darling son. But there is something that even You cannot take from me— my faith in You!"

We need this kind of soul-power to face life's lowest moments on the highest levels.

DO IT NOW

Maybe you've a friend who attempted complimenting you with the exclamation:

"My, but you haven't changed in years!"

It's not such a good compliment.

As the years fly away, we get ourselves into ruts and grooves which wind up in dead ends. Somehow you hear people saying today who said fifteen years ago:

"One day I will slow down, reduce my activities, and take time out to get to know my children."

This, added to a host of other deferred debts to themselves and their families.

We are plagued by the "disease of manana"! But today is all we now have. Yesterday has fled and tomorrow is still beyond us.

Few of us, if any, postpone our material considerations. We work today to eat today and tomorrow. But we often postpone our spiritual acquisitions to the tomorrow that never comes. The books we said we would read, the friends we would acquire, the love we would give, the helping hand we would offer. Or the God we would seek and know.

But we really postpone nothing, for every delay constitutes a decision. Every time we decide to wait for tomorrow we neglect to do what we should do today.

As we grow wiser we realize that what counts most are our spiritual resources. We seek to fall back upon them in the hours of our deepest need. But we have been duped by our own delusion. We have no bank balance. We cannot have a spiritual account any time in our later life, when through the years we've neglected making regular deposits.

We ought to remember:

If someone is waiting for our love, our smile, and our devotion, we had better offer them now. Our beloved may not be here tomorrow!

If deep within us there is a gratitude which needs to be expressed, a spiritual debt that needs to be paid, we had better "do it now!"

The life of confidence begins at the beginning; it always begins now. "Now or Never" is more than a catchword phrase: it is the product of mature observation of human nature at work.

For he who does not do now what must now be done, will never do!

DON'T NEGLECT TODAY

In a small town in New York, traffic officers put up a sign on a drive which wound through a park. It read: "This road does not lead anywhere very rapidly. If you are in a hurry, you are on the wrong road."

Thereby hangs a tell-tale sign of our times.

What makes Sammy, Johnny, or Freddy run? They are all dressed up, going nowhere, yet obviously in a hurry to get there. The mad tempo of our lives is often but a cover-up for their lack of meaning; we insist on running long after the race has been lost. And the pity: We imagine ourselves the victors.

Possessing such strenuous and sometimes wild timetables, we soon discover that we have run out of time to do many good and happy things.

"I wish I had the time for that", we piously declaim when confronted with simple pleasures or duties. The unabashed truth is to the contrary: We do have time, we are bored by simplicity; we refuse to ride a slow road.

Time has a way of running out on us, playing tricks on even the most unsuspecting.

Too often we spend so much effort preparing for what's to come, that we never get to enjoy each day's blessings. A host of lives have been wasted anticipating the future without making the most of the "everlasting now". We need to learn how to look ahead, but never overlook today in looking over tomorrow.

Before we cross the tracks to our never-never land, we've got to stop, look, and listen to the call of the hour here and now.

In search of the rainbow at the edge of the horizon, many a man has lost his way in life. For a man who is seeking everything ends up with nothing if he's never satisfied with something.

To illustrate, here is the story of a poor woman who now knows better. She received an egg as a gift for her sick child.

"Mother, may I have the egg?" the boy cried out. "I'm hungry."

"No, my son", she replied. "We must keep an eye to the future. We'll save the egg."

"But what will we do with the egg?"

"We will ask our good neighbour to let her hen sit on our egg until it hatches into a chicken."

"Then shall we have chicken to eat?"

"No, my child. We must think of the future. We will keep the chicken until it grows and begins to lay eggs."

"Then we'll have *lots* of eggs to eat."

"No, not so fast", replied the mother. "We shall gather the eggs together and have our chicken sit on them until they all hatch into many more chickens."

"Then we'll really be able to eat chicken as often as we like, won't we, Mother?"

"Not if we are to think of the future.   We will sell some of the chickens and buy a calf, which we will raise until it is a cow. Eventually the cow will have calves, some of which we will raise and sell to buy a field.   Just imagine, my son, how rich we shall become!   We'll have a field with cows, with calves, with chickens, and with eggs—and all from this one, small egg!"

The woman became so excited at the thought of future riches that she clapped her hands with joy.   But, alas!—in so doing, she smashed the little egg.

Counting her chickens before they were hatched, she never got to enjoy what she did have.   And thinking only of what we are going to do, we neglect to do what we should be doing. We've got to be prepared.   Not for tomorrow alone, but for today as well.

So dream your dreams, pursue your visions, and set your sights high and wide.   But never barter this day for another. Right now, it's all you have.

DON'T OVERLOOK TOMORROW

Though today is all you have, keep your eye on tomorrow.

We need microscopes to see clearly what faces us now.   Yet sometimes we suffer from an overdose of "now-ism".   We become so pre-occupied with the trivial minutiae of the moment that we never muster enough confidence to reach out for the greater tomorrows.

This is why we also need telescopes.   We need a vision of what's ahead of us.   Though they seem to be hidden by dark clouds of doubt and fear, we've got to focus our sights on the remote peaks which beckon.

Real spiritual strength and wholesome confidence in life's aspiring quality are the products of the wisdom which recognizes that today and tomorrow are twins—Siamese twins, at that.

There once was a man named Tycho Brahe. He was born in Denmark and educated at the University of Copenhagen. At first he thought of studying law, but then decided to study astronomy. In the course of his work, while yet a young man, he discovered a new star, and this spread his fame at home and abroad.

Denmark then had a king who was a patron of learning, and the king built an observatory for Tycho at the centre of a little island, and Tycho called the place Uraniborg—the City of the Heavens.

Here, for years and years he worked, by day and night, till star after star, with exquisite precision, had been set down upon his chart.

But Frederick the king died and young Prince Christian came upon the throne. The new king grudged the treasure that had been lavished upon the upkeep of the observatory. He could not see the value of it all. He immediately dispatched messengers to question Tycho, to learn the use of all his labour, and to pit their values against his.

The story is set forth brilliantly in a poem by Alfred Noyes— *Watchers of the Skies*. The messengers asked Tycho what he had been doing these five and twenty years. He showed them tables of the stars, 700 set down, each in its proper place.

"And is this all?" they said. "Not all, I hope," said Tycho, "for I think before I die I shall have marked a thousand."

You can almost hear their laughter, can you not? All the prophets and leaders have listened to the same. Einstein had heard it in our day, and every man who has loved truth and beauty, every man who has seen visions and tried to live them in his life, has heard the same sardonic mirth.

"To what end," said the messengers, "to what end, the travail and the waste? Show its use to us now, show it now before we go."

There has never been a philosopher, a prophet, a scientist, or an artist who has not been summoned to a similar proof. Prove to us its value today! Not the value for the world of tomorrow—but today!

Tycho gave his answer:

"Year after year, we patiently record all we can gather. In some far-off time a people that we have not known shall hear the stars moving like music to a single end."

But the messengers could not understand. They went back to the king and said that Tycho Brahe's dreams were fruitless, and, worse than fruitless, they were perilous, since "any fruit they bore would fall in distant years to alien hands." Tycho Brahe went forth into exile, and Uraniborg, City of the Heavens, went down into dust. Tycho said:

"Yet, I still hope to make my 1,000 before I die. Little enough I know—a midget's work; but the men that follow me with more delicate art will be saved just that five and twenty years of patience, and be brought sooner to the goal of that Kingdom of the Law which I shall not see.

"Theirs be the palms, the shouting, and the praise. Ours be the father's glory in the sons."

Part II

BE A
CONFIDENT
PERSON

KNOW HOW TO WORK

Most people think of Bible stories as tales intended for young children. As a result, few adults know the real significance of the Bible, in spite of the fact that they can easily recount sweet recollections of childhood fantasies.

But the Bible is a library of books which requires serious study and deep scrutiny on the part of men who would be mature. Its stories are often expressed in what has been called "the forgotten language"—the vocabulary of symbol and ethical suggestion.

Consider the tale of Noah and the ark, as example. The average adult thinks only of a man and his family, crowded into a tiny boat, surrounded by a teeming mass of elephants, giraffes, and assorted members of the animal kingdom. Indeed, the more vivid our childhood memories of the legendary side of the story, the greater the possibility that, as adults, we shall think of Noah and the ark in immature ways.

The sages of the Talmud recognized this possibility. That is why they went beyond the literal tale of Noah and other Biblical heroes, and sought to discover the adult significance: They looked for the inner meaning of the symbol and the ethical purpose of the narrative.

They suggested that Noah spent a whole lifetime building the ark on dry land. As he built it, scoffers came to view his "foolish" labour, to poke fun and jest.

"Why this fantastic effort, Noah?" they jibed. "Why build an ark", they mocked, "when there is no water?" But Noah remained undeterred. He saw what was on the horizon; his neighbours could only see what was under their noses. He laboured for tomorrow; his friends thought only of the moment.

Here is a significant lesson for those who spend their zealous energies only on things which "bring immediate results". Failing to achieve sudden success, we turn away from important responsibilities to quick, facile, but empty trivia.

There are always those who are impatient with their speed and want to arrive at life's goals more quickly. They seek the short cuts which appear alluring, but which are often wasteful. Shortening the time it takes to reach a goal is no guarantee that we shall ever reach it.

Often, after a whole lifetime, some wake up to discover that while they have been working very hard, their labour has been in vain because it was linked only to the need of the moment, to the gratification of the passing hour.

Noah was different. He was different because he laboured patiently, with maturity. Children need to find their efforts crowned with immediate reward or else they have no desire to continue their work. Why? Because they are children! They are dominated by the immature need for swift and easy gratification. A child cannot be a Noah!

Young people, and older ones who never grew up, forget that Nature has foreordained that time is required for healing, understanding, or maturity. But they want desperately to hasten the process. They pull open a rosebud and wilfully demand to extract a full-grown rose. Yet, the processes of Nature will not be hurried. The well-tempered, slow-ripened fruit of the field is hardier and sturdier than the hot-house product.

To be a Noah we need to see what looms on the horizon and dedicate our labour to what we see, in spite of the "blind" scoffers who will not see. To be a Noah we need moral backbone to face up to the derisive noise of the crowd. To be a

Noah we must refuse to be moulded into conforming, common-place stereotypes by the convictions of weak people.

The confident man knows how to work: he is patient and deliberate.   He applies regular and consistent effort to the tasks of life.   He works while others merely talk.   He can still walk ahead while others are tired from running.

MAKE CONSTANT EFFORT

"Do it yourself!"   You, too, have probably been caught up in the fad that is sweeping the country.

Tired businessmen and harried housewives are building a wide variety of household objects in their hours of leisure. Chairs, wall cases, and asphalt-tile floors have their uses.   But once upon a time, legend has it, there were bigger stakes at hand.

When King Solomon was about to erect his temple, he invited all his people to help him.   Everyone was offered the opportunity to take part in its construction.   The people were divided into a number of groups—the wise men, the priests, the mighty men, and the poor.

The wise men chose to build the southern wall.   But they were too busy thinking about life, and so they sent their slaves.   The priests asked permission to construct the northern wall.   But they were involved in their own ministry, and so they sent their servants instead.

The men of means and prestige sought to build the eastern wall.   But they had not time for it.   They, too, sent their slaves.

One wall remained—the western wall.   The poor were granted permission to build it.   With great joy they "did it themselves".

When the temple was destroyed, the legend continues, all walls crumbled—all but one. Indeed, if you visit Jerusalem today you can still see the western wall, the lone rampart that remains.

Eloquent reminder, the story suggests, of something we regularly neglect. Read all you want about swimming, cooking, or driving and you are still left untried. Someone said correctly that we learn best by doing. To know how to swim you have to get into the water yourself and swim.

The truth applies with equal force to the life of our spirit. No psychologist or pediatrician can bring up your children for you. The deep, the wonderful things in life—love and hope, loyalty, courage, and confidence—cannot be achieved for us by others.

Charity does not consist of signing a cheque, but of giving something of ourselves. Social progress does not come about simply by reading or thinking about it. It is achieved by the "doers", not the "sayers".

We get out of life only what we give of ourselves. And no one else can talk us into "how to live" or "how to do it". There just is no substitute for our own doing, our own living.

ACCEPT NEW IDEAS

Interior decorators are fine people. I have no quarrel with them, but they ought not to decide what books will line our shelves.

Things probably are not that bad; they only seem that way. Yet, more and more homes give the unhappy impression that what few books they do contain are not chosen for reading. As the visitor casts an eye over the shelves, he gets the feeling that the books and book jackets were chosen with a careful regard for the colour scheme of the room.

In this television age, the art of reading is, for many, relegated to the archaeological past. Many of our homes seem nothing more than display cases in which much is on view, but little is discussed, analyzed, or thought through.

There is no substitute for good reading. Audio-visual aids such as movies and film strips may be useful classroom techniques, but they do not, alone, produce the educated man. We still are wondering about some of the "ninety-day wonders" the army "educated" in haste in World War II. You can "train" an animal in ninety days, but you cannot educate it. And so with humans.

The purpose of education goes far beyond the acquisition of techniques and hastily memorized skills. Its purpose is to put us in touch with great ideas: ideas that can help change our lives for the better.

Ideas come down to us from the past and are distilled in the minds of great men who have reacted to them in their own unique way. Even as the glaciers leave their imprints on the sands of time, so these men have bequeathed to us their reactions to life in the thrilling, throbbing, stimulating, and surprising words they have put into books.

The trouble, it seems, with many so-called "educated" people is that they once read a book and never got over it. Truth to tell, most college graduates in North America are "super-kindergarteners", who have not even begun to learn how to learn. Dr. George Gallup once wisely suggested: "Let colleges wait twenty-five years after graduation before awarding degrees." Only then, he observed, could a student give sufficient proof that he had continued earnestly and systematically to pursue his interest in learning and had continued to develop mentally and spiritually.

Wisdom ripens slowly. Very few really achieve its fruits, because they imagine they have it when they have not: They confuse information with insight. Wisdom is built upon the foundation stone of knowledge—but it is more than knowledge. And even knowledge does not consist in what you once learned; rather is it the broad total of what you have unlearned, relearned, and newly-learned. Above all, real wisdom begins when we get to know how much we do not know.

To be truly educated means to be open to new challenges of thought—all the time.

We require the ability to sit down quietly and make friends with new books—all the time.

Confidence in our own beliefs and opinions should not make iron-clad robots of us. We need to have faith in the ultimate values, together with a willingness to expose ourselves to the risk of re-thinking our accepted conventions—all the time!

A charitable person is not someone who once gave money to a noble cause. It is a person of sensitive character and conscience, with a continuing sense of obligation.

With truly educated persons it is not what they once knew that counts, but rather their willingness to search out the old ideas they've missed and the new ideas still a-borning.

SEE ROOM FOR IMPROVEMENT

Improvement or perfection.

Take your choice, you cannot have both.

A man who picks the perfect world, the perfect community, the perfect arrangement of human life never comes even close. He ends up rebelling against his ideals, bereft of a purpose, morbid, despairing. Often he becomes a rebel without a cause.

Quite other is the man who seeks to improve life, in the little as well as in the larger issues. He faces live options, vital possibilities. He may not be able to perfect the world, but he can still try to change it.

The trouble with many of us moderns is our faulty idealism. We get excited about saving the world, but spurn the thought of improving ourselves. We are enthusiastic over great and massive utopias, but neglect to bother with the means to the ends. After all, we tell ourselves, we can't be interested in details, when we are busy with the grand idea and the total hope.

But faith and hope, like charity, must begin at home. One may not necessarily accept Hindu religion or the orthodoxies of the Christian or Jewish faiths. Yet they have a strength to teach, and a power to impart. Their adherents have learned the meaning of personal discipline. Just as the body is built up through physical exercise, so the spirit of man requires rigorous attention. Religion thus deals with means as well as ends, with the self as well as with the world. And what is more: it knows that failure is as important as success. While religion may not supply us with all of the answers to our problems, it does teach us how to look at the problems. And it urges us to bother very much with the means and the methods.

Being concerned with the details, religion helps create in us what we really need—the personal discipline that leads to self-improvement. When we accept the job of improving our own world, we go to the world at large with a little more humility and a lot more perspective. We may then be willing to struggle longer and harder to improve the world, instead of turning our backs upon it when we fail to perfect it.

So let us teach our hearts to be patient, to struggle and grapple with our lower selves without let-up.

And above all, remember: Each day opens up a new world and gives us a chance at making a new beginning.

KNOW HOW TO LOSE
IN ORDER TO WIN

"Be a sport!"

Sometimes I wish that more people would take seriously this wonderful suggestion that is so freely heard today.   It is a thought that reflects the spirit of North America so well.   But too often we lose sight of its real meaning for our own spiritual lives.

To "be a sport" one has to know how to play.   And in the greatest game of skill—the adventure of life—there are altogether too many people who don't know the rules of the game.

The first and foremost rule is very simple.   It is just this: You can't win all the time, so better learn how to lose.

Babe Ruth was the home run king of his day, but don't forget how often he used to strike out.   Nor has any major league baseball player concluded a full season with much more than one out of three safe hits to his credit.   There is no real game of skill in which even the most expert can consistently achieve a perfect score.

One of the most common ailments of our day is "perfection-itis".   Those who suffer from it keep punishing themselves mercilessly for not doing what can't be done in the first place.

There is a big difference between wanting to improve ourselves and wanting to be absolutely perfect.   The former is perfectly natural and human and therefore constructive.   The latter is an example of man playing the god, and it can be dangerous, even destructive.

One can understand the artist who continues to paint his picture over and over to come closer to his ideal. Or the author who polishes and brightens up his prose so that his real spirit can shine through more clearly. But when an artist and author linger for a lifetime upon a single work because they are obsessed with the need for perfection, rarely do they contribute anything of lasting significance.

What is more: They often have not even learned how to improve. And this for the simple reason that to improve you have to learn how to fail.

Henry Ford forgot to put a reverse gear into his first automobile. If he had striven for perfection, he may never have known enough to improve the automobiles that he built later.

There is something else wrong with the fellow who follows the line of "everything-or-nothing". He is critical of himself because he's made some mistakes, and will never venture forth because he's gripped by fear of doing the wrong thing. But let's test his thinking. For a moment, let's suppose that he's right: that one should strive to be perfect because this is the great ideal of life.

What happens when you achieve the ideal? Is this the end of the matter? The moment you've fooled yourself into believing that you have achieved the ideal, you've really lost it! Indeed, the ideal is not a station you arrive at in life. Rather, it's a way of travelling through life.

All of which suggests that to win we've got to learn to lose. And we've also got to learn the difference between a single inning and the whole game.

Moses never got to the Promised Land. He died at the mountain top, but never entered the land. He was no failure, but a significant success. He didn't get there, but the children of Israel did.

Perhaps this is just what some of us need to remember about ourselves. We can't achieve everything we set out to achieve. But we can get closer to it. And when we don't run away from the challenge, we make it possible for our children to achieve.

SEE OPPORTUNITIES IN CRISES

Crisis calls out the true nature of a man. A man is what he proves to be in response to trouble.

There are many people whose disorganized views of life stand out in bold relief when they are confronted with sudden emergency. They have a feet-first, head-last response.

Only suddenly do they become aware of what has been apparent for along time. They cannot see things as they develop. They can only act when the ship is burning. And then, only precipitously!

Recall Gideon! This Hebrew warrior commanded a force of barely 300 men against the mighty Midianites, yet he was victorious. Each of his men took a ram's horn in hand and blasted notes of alarm. The Midianites responded with confusion. They were thrown into a state of shock.

The alarm of crisis brought forth no new powers from within them. Thrown into disorder and frenzy they set their swords against their own brothers.

Modern Midianites abound. Many of us lack foresight and often refuse to see what is happening. We postpone making decisions until terror strikes. Then, frightened into action, we move swiftly but heedlessly into the fray. But speed without direction is meaningless. Sometimes, as the Midianites, we succeed only in destroying ourselves.

Some people erroneously believe that it is all a matter of education. An educated person, they say, will know how to face a crisis.

Education is of value but it is only a tool. It helps a man to use his education in order to mobilize his inner, human resources. A lot of educated people have lost their heads when they needed them most, because they never realized that they needed more than a head.

In the Chinese language the word for crisis is written in two characters, the first meaning "danger", the second "opportunity".

What a profound understanding of all of life we could have if we saw it as *danger offering opportunity*.

Only a virile religious outlook can help us see life this way. We are made aware that every moment is a moment of decision, every day a day of commitment.

The man without spiritual mooring floats through life as driftwood, and when crisis comes he must run away. He can only lose because he can only hesitate.

BEND WITH THE BLOWS

Morals teachers are wont to interpret the physical elements of life as spiritual opportunities. They have been known to explain man's possession of two eyes as a lesson in good living: with one eye we should see things as they are, with the other as they should be. Or man's two ears. Here, too, a lesson: with one, listen for the good, with the other reject the evil. And why one mouth? To remind us forever that truth is one and indivisible: what we think we ought to say, what we say we ought to think.

One can go on to seek further moral meaning from man's physical frame. Let's talk about bones—wishbones, jawbones, and backbones.

Some people there are who are all wishbone. Their lives consist of a continuous round of day-dreaming and open-eyed fantasy. They need to remember that to wish is not the same as to hope.

Real optimism has its roots in painful experience, in the deeper knowledge that comes from failure. It seeks the best but is ready for the worst. It remains victorious and unconquered even in defeat. It can try and yet not be tried. For it will try again.

But he who is filled up with just the vapid wish never ventures forth, never takes the step that leads to the hope that can conquer defeat. He is just wish-washy.

And from the wishbone to the jawbone is but one, short, fruitless step. Wishing may be costly, may reduce our real potential at the price of inertia, but talk is cheap.

We glibly mouth empty words and often become intoxicated with sounds and furies signifying nothing. We talk about life instead of living. We settle for sweet syllables, overworking our jawbones and forgetting our backbones.

Man's real stature is measured by how high he stands, how much he can withstand, how firmly he remains planted when the big winds come.

He can bend with the blows but never be bowed down. He will have as much solid ground under him as there is starry heaven above him. He will not just talk, but speak out and up.

For he will come to know that he can stand up only as long as he stands for something. No bones about it, backbone is really character compounded with courage and conscience!

ACCEPT THE RESPONSIBILITY
OF FREEDOM

There were several groups, legend has it, that stood before the Red Sea's surging surf in Pharaoh's Egypt.

These were men, recall, who were about to be liberated from a long and heavy bondage. They should have been united by the hope of a new freedom.

They should have been thrilled by their opportunity. But many were still enthralled by their own small fears. They were paralyzed by fright. Ironically, some men will prefer the ease of slavery to freedom. They are overwhelmed by the added duties, responsibilities, and spiritual exertions which human liberty requires.

So it was that one of these groups counselled friends to return to Egypt as the best way to avoid "taking the plunge" into freedom. We still hear echoes of this cry down to our day. There are many who, in their personal lives or in their national outlook, cannot face up to the challenge of decision-making for today. They can only retreat, singing hymns to the "good old times" while lamenting the birth of a new day.

Frenzy gripped the others when they saw the Egyptians after them in hot pursuit. They made no real decision. They literally jumped to their conclusions. Some drowned themselves.

Our ears still pick up these sounds of frightened, frantic men. Men who fall prey to the camouflaged perils of the path of least immediate resistance.

They act like heroes but think like cowards, for their jittery fears betray them.

They are persuaded into believing that destruction paves the way to peace.   But it can no more achieve this than self-destruction can make for life.

It is no accident that all of these people were looking the wrong way.   They faced Egypt.   Their backs were turned on the land of promise.   Nor do we today remember any of them.   They are part of the nameless oblivion of the legions of fear that have blocked the doors of hope.

One man we do remember.   We remember him because he didn't succumb to the cowardly chatter of those noisy nobodies.   He faced a different way.   He spoke a different word.   He said: "Let us go forward!"   This forward faith had something to do with the miracle of the waters dividing.

And every time we look to the promised land and find the courage to face our future, similar miracles can take place for each of us.

FACE YOUR TROUBLES

Sinbad the Sailor was under the impression that he had found a good place to anchor.

He discovered to his surprise that what he thought was an island was only a beast of the sea.   His boat, of course, was not anchored but went charging off in all directions.

Like Sinbad, we hold on to many things which do not hold on to us, and we are easily upended in a stormy sea.   For the trouble with us *is* trouble.   Some of us are undone by trouble; still others are troublemakers.   But there are those whom trouble makes.   The Psalmist has a phrase for them: "Passing through the valley of weeping, they make it a place of springs."   This is the kind of man a man ought to try to be.

Too often we seek the comfortable answers which lead to soft spots. We're afraid of the rough edges. We want to cuddle up into a cozy corner and shut out the world.

But we become smug when we're snug. And when life's shafts begin to fall around us we're faint-hearted when we should be tough-minded. The easy way turns out to be the longest way.

For it is not so much what happens to us that counts as the way we take it. Not what we find in life but what we do with what we find makes us men. The real question is not: "What's happened to me?" Rather it is: "What am I making of it?"

There are two ways we can meet life's difficulties. We can look for excuses and alibis, blaming our troubles for our cowardice; we can pass the buck, criticizing the times we live in for our own inner chaos and confusion. This is the way we go to pieces, because we don't see life whole.

But the man who does see life whole knows that crisis is the raw material out of which good character and conduct are made. We never learn to toughen up our "spiritual muscles", never gain the inner confidence we need to meet life "head-on" if we seek ease and run away from trouble.

One never finds life pre-fabricated. All one finds is raw material. Sometimes it is rough and tough, ungainly and unpromising, but in the hands of courageous and dedicated men it can be made into a thing of beauty and meaning.

We're not the first generation to face trouble in such vast amounts. Indeed, there has never been a great man who wasn't the product of a tough time. The darkest hours of human civilization have been among the most creative.

Some of the world's great spirits made history just when everyone else thought that it was coming to an end.

After the flood there comes the rainbow—but only to those who have seen it shining through the storm.

UNDERSTAND THE VALUE OF DREAMS

Someone asked his friend:

"If you were shipwrecked, alone, on a far-away island, and could have one book, what one would you choose?"

He got a ready answer. His friend replied:

"Johnson's Manual of Ship Building!"

We live in such a practical world that many of the things we want or have, represent our driving desire for physical necessity or luxury, and nothing more.

To be sure, we need the practical man. Without him we would lack the elementary necessities of clothing, food, and shelter.

But what's a house if it isn't a home? And what's a school if it isn't a sanctuary? Or what's a world without a dream?

Leave the world to practical men only and imagine what would happen. There could be no love, no deep devotion, no abiding loyalties.

All of life would be reduced to a single question: "What's in it for me?"

Western civilization has brought much of value to the world. Through it, many diseases have been conquered, many human blights eradicated. Great buildings and cities have been erected by man's technical skills. Going forward materially, we also imagine that the only standards by which things, ideas, and men are to be judged are those which evaluate production and the quick result.

More than we realize, our homes, communities, and nations depend upon ideals and not things. No gadget or device can take the place of hope and the faith of the human heart.

Even generals on the field of battle, armed with the most advanced equipment, cannot win when their soldiers do not believe in what they are doing.

Ironically, a scientific age should have produced a more spiritually-patient age. When Edison's colleagues were about to give up after 50,000 attempts in their search for the successful experiment, they turned to him in despair and said: "We have laboured in vain. We know nothing!" Edison turned upon them, still aglow with the spirit that transcends the visible, that passes from the known into the unknown, and replied: "You are wrong, my friends. We have made 50,000 experiments. You think that they have failed. Perhaps. I believe that they have succeeded! We now know 50,000 ways that won't work."

It is not only important to learn from our immediate success, but even more instructive to learn from our failures. But with one basic precaution: We must never allow ourselves to succumb to failures by calling them successes. If we are impatient, we will vulgarize our search and be satisfied to stop with failures, making believe that they are successes.

Someone has aptly said: If we are not idealistic, perhaps even radical, at the age of twenty, there is something wrong with our hearts; if we are not realistically practical at the age of sixty, there is something wrong with our heads.

Yet, in order to come to the fulness of life armed with the power to meet life's challenges, we need to bring to our years some of the qualities of courage we have developed as young people.

If once we did know how to dream, we can at least face older age with philosophical perspective, and the balanced wisdom of years brightly spent.

Joseph the dreamer was able to interpret Pharaoh's visions. For only a dreamer can understand, appreciate, and value the beauty and the power of someone else's dreams.

Everybody, whether aware of it or not, has a religion. Everyone has a God. There is one major difference. Some believe in a god of things—of fine houses, factories, cars, and machines. Their god is the God of Success—the success of the moment. Others commit their lives to a non-practical, unseen, untouched, unheard of value—the spirit which hovers over all things. They know the value of dreams.

It is faith in a spiritual, higher power which can give us that spirit of confidence in our inner power necessary to change houses into homes, family tables into altars, schools and offices into sanctuaries.

FEEL THAT IT'S ALL WORTHWHILE

The greatest gift you can ever give is the gift of yourself— therefore, shut out the noise of the world and begin working on your own rough edges!

This is a lesson learned from the life of David, the father, and Solomon, the son.

Solomon's wisdom brought forth an era of peace and prosperity; thus, he could more easily build the Temple unto the Lord. Solomon built the Temple; but it was David's idea; his dream, his hope.

David lived in times more perilous. The shepherd and sweet singer had to become the warrior and defender.

The Temple of Solomon, however, is first and foremost the House of David. Never privileged to build it, no longer alive to see it, it was yet David who was its real builder. To Solomon he gave the inspiration to do what he wanted to do but could not.

We are, many of us, not unlike David. We, too, are constrained not to do many things we would want to do, because of circumstances and situations which are beyond control.   We dream, but often the hard realities of life destroy our real purposes and deny us our deepest fulfillments.   We never seem to be able to touch the sacred soil of our promised lands; we can only dimly perceive them from afar.

In a profound sense, however, David did build the Temple. The paradox of human existence, the Bible suggests, is not resolved through what we ourselves may personally achieve, but rather through the immortality of our influence—the manner in which the spirit of our lives abides in lives we have shaped and moulded.

This is the eternal problem of every teacher, every parent, every thoughtful person.   How can we justify our lives?   How may we find blessing for all of our travail, our hard and bitter labours which go unfulfilled?   The answers come only with maturity.   Teachers go on teaching, scientists searching, parents loving, in the fervent belief that their own lives may yet be justified in the lives of others whose hearts and minds they will touch and exalt.

Others may waiver, may scoff, may sit on their hands. The way to confidence, in spite of travail, is reached by those who
  a)   learn to work by making constant effort,
  b)   accept new ideas with a courage born of enthusiasm for living,
  c)   seek to learn from failure, by making crises into opportunities for growth,
  d)   face trouble as a natural part of life, because they know themselves to be free men who must make free choices, and
  e)   hold tightly the ideals cherished in their youth and boldly continue to dream.

"Who is the hero?" asked an ancient sage. And he answered: "He who masters himself!"   We may not get to the land of promise except through the lives of those we influence. But how shall we influence others if we do not first become worthy of emulation? We shall be heroes for others when we are confident of our own promise, our own power.

Part III

BEGIN
WITH
YOURSELF

O, LORD, BEGIN WITH ME!

A story is told of disciples of a saintly rabbi who were troubled by the prevalence of evil in the world. They came to their rabbi desirous of learning how to drive out the forces of darkness.

The rabbi listened to their plaint and suggested to his students that they descend into the cellar of the house and take brooms in their hands and try to sweep the darkness from the cellar.

Amazed, they nevertheless obliged their learned teacher and complied with his suggestion. After a number of hours of futile effort, they returned to their teacher and told of the failure of their work.

The rabbi then suggested another remedy to his students: "Take sticks in your hands and descend again into the darkness and drive it out with the sticks."

Again, they followed the rabbi's advice. Once more their effort was of no avail.

When they returned to tell him of their second failure, the rabbi turned to them with this final suggestion: "My children, perhaps you can better meet the challenge of darkness if each of you will descend into the cellar and light your own candle. See if this avails!"

They went to the cellar, kindled their candles, and behold, the darkness was driven out!

That rabbi was certain that the world needed to be saved; but he was also certain that one of the ways of saving the world was through self-improvement. He was telling his students:

You drive out the darkness around you by illuminating a light within you.

It is of little or no avail to complain of our bad fate, or of our thorny trials.   Real strength is the slow product of the energy we apply to our own rough edges.   Too often the tears of self-pity blind our eyes from seeing ourselves in proper perspective.

We could be happy heroes and not hapless victims if we learned to flex our spiritual muscles to combat inertia.

We sit on our hands, bemoaning our fate when in fact it is not our fate but our faith that is poor.   If we had the courage that is born of an inner light, we could solve our biggest problems—ourselves!

Instead of fighting windmills, we need to conquer ourselves. If we were truly in earnest about saving the world, we would spend less time criticizing those who disagree with us, more time learning how to perfect our own character.

There always have been two major approaches to human welfare.   The one starts with society, with the environment, with the group in which we live.   This approach has produced outstanding reformers, dreamers, and idealists whose passion for the good life finds expression in many of the great passages of our holy scriptures, and in the remarkable documents of free societies everywhere.

The other approach is less dramatic but not one whit less significant.   It is based on the thought that no society or community can rise higher than the level of its individual constituents.

We may talk a good deal about freedom as a social goal, but unless freedom is a living, personal reality it means nothing in the abstract.

Indeed, we often are quite heroic about our social goals, even zealously active in communal efforts for group welfare, and all the while we neglect cultivating these very qualities in our own lives and in the lives of our children.

There are too many people who lead communities but whose personal lives, either in thought or in practice, do not reflect their social goals.

How many people do we know who are always ready to attend meetings dealing with social problems, but seem oblivious to their own deep, inner needs and the similar needs of their families?

There are many altars that lead to a sanctified life. But none so significant as the altar of the self.

We suggest to some would-be do-gooders that widely-known petition: O, Lord, change the world—and begin with me!

YOU HAVE IT WITHIN YOU

Security. If you asked the average man to sum up his life's greatest desire that would be his word for it.

You'll find, of course, many re-arrangements and combinations. But always you come back to the same word: Social security, job security, old-age security, wage security.

Where does security come from? Is it a physical thing?

The Chinese thought it resided in a Great Wall; the French, in a Maginot Line; and we think of it in the form of a bomb.

History has something to say about that kind of security. It reminds us that these are only the things men use to cover up their fears, suits of mail that cloak shivering spines. But they offer no real security.

Nor does security come from passing a law, or from political systems that promise quick, special delivery of their brand of pie in the sky.

Money is security, others will say. There's a half-truth, if ever there was one! Certainly money helps give us the impression that all is well, that we can get and do whatever we want. But dig down deep into your own self and ask yourself if you've been kept happy for long by things money can buy.

We need many material things. But we'd live as happily and maybe more nobly without a good many of them. Money matters, but not supremely. Money may make us men of means, but not of ends. Nor do we achieve security by confusing the two.

There once was a fox, so a legend has it, which found a vineyard that was fenced on all sides. There was just one hole. He wished to enter through it, but was unable to do so. What did he do? He fasted three days, until he became very thin, and then went through the small opening. He feasted then and, of course, grew fat again. When he wanted to go out, he was unable to pass through the hole. So he fasted another three days until he had grown quite thin. Then he went out.

When he was outside, he turned and said:

"O vineyard! What use have you been to me and what use are your fruits? All that is inside is beautiful, but of what benefit? As one enters so one comes out."

When a person enters the world, his fingers are clenched, as though to say, "Everything is mine." When he departs from the world, his hands are open, as though to say, "I have acquired nothing."

To be sure, we need protection from the physical dangers of life. Every man has a right to live so that none can make him afraid.

But security that begins and ends by the measure of what our hands can grab or acquire, or by what shelters our back, misses the point.

The heart of the matter is a matter of the heart. Real security begins and ends as a supreme inner buoyancy, a built-in faith that lifts us up to face every trial. It is within us or it is nowhere.

YOU NEED HELP FOR SELF-HELP

Did you ever get a splinter in your hand or a cinder in your eye?

Then you know how nervous and ill at ease you felt when someone else had to dig it out for you. And yet when you youself went after the disturbing element, you did not feel hurt.

Here is a valuable principle in the cure of many of our private problems. Self-help, in the long run, is the only way to fight our fears and destroy our phobias.

Yet we often walk around, burdened with overwhelming stresses. We are caught in a confusing dilemma.

We don't go to our doctor or to our clergyman because we're too embarrassed to tell another about ourselves, afraid to expose our bareness to the light of another's eyes.

On the other hand, we can't carry our overload. Our emotional knees buckle under the strain.

But when we find ourselves burdened so, we should go to someone who can help us. And how are we helped best? When we are shown how to help ourselves.

More often than not, a counsellor or a friend serves best when he gives us a chance to get things off our chest, to air out the smoldering fires that consume us.

Sometimes this in itself is a therapy. For our tensions tighten us up, and we need to be unshackled by unravelling our home-made chains.

Thus it is that a good friend, a helper in need, must first be a good listener.   That's why all of us like people who are willing to hear us out, who give us an opportunity to be listened to.

There are some husbands and wives that I know who have been speaking to each other for a long time, but neither the husbands nor the wives have been listening.   And parents, too, might remember that their children also are anxious to be heard sometimes.

Once our story has been told and we have put out our fears in the light of day, we must understand that no one can help us if we don't help ourselves.

Every prayer, every wish, every hope must be directed to making ourselves capable of self-help.   For even God doesn't help those who won't help themselves.

FEEL THOUGHTFULLY!
THINK FEELINGLY!

"The heart has its reasons which reason does not know."

Pascal's profound insight into human understanding has been a helpful antidote to some extremist thinking on the subject of science, philosophy, and religion.

But it is a thought which also throws light elsewhere—on some of our personal vices.

Too often, we overlook the role of good, sound sentiment. We gloss over our feelings, refuse to give them real ventilation, afraid that we may be accused of being emotional. But without virile emotions, naturally expressed, life would be dull and robot-like.   We would give up being ourselves for fear of "giving ourselves away".

After all, to a great extent, we are what we feel. And if we consciously freeze out our feelings, we become counterfeit, false, and other than we really are. True respect and admiration come only to those who genuinely express what they are, not to those who seek to impress by appearing to be what they are not.

A leopard cannot change his spots, nor need he. He will always be a leopard. To be men we need only act like men, and we'll be accepted for what we are.

But while we ought always express and never repress our feelings, we should never hide behind them. Sometimes we delude ourselves into believing that we feel something we don't feel at all. We refuse to do what reason tells us is right because we fear the consequences of doing what we know we should do. So we protect our ego by proclaiming—"I have my reasons."

But these turn out to be neither reasonable nor rational.

When pushed to explain, we retreat by saying: "Look. I don't have to have any reasons. I just feel that way."

In our daily pursuits we accumulate a large backlog of "reasons" for not doing the things which reason would require us to do. We have "reasons" which are no reasons and "feelings" which we've never really felt.

Human beings are feeling and thinking creatures. They need to feel thoughtfully and think feelingly. And they must do both honestly and naturally.

BUILD UP YOUR WILL POWER

Prominent and successful in his community, a gentleman had placed this description of his philosophy on his desk: "Success is a ladder of ten rungs. Some scale it in one fell swoop. Others, slowly but surely. But some get caught in mid-air; they never climb higher." Beneath this introduction, there was a picture of a ladder; the lowest rung was valued at 10 per cent while the highest was equal to 100 per cent:

    10 per cent— I can't.
    20 per cent—I don't know.
    30 per cent—I wish I could.
    40 per cent—I could.
    50 per cent—I think I might.
    60 per cent—I might.
    70 per cent—I think I can.
    80 per cent—I can.
    90 per cent—I will.
    100 per cent—I did.

Very few of us reach the 100 per cent rung, because we've gotten lost on the way and never touch the 90 per cent mark. There is very little that stands in the way of a man's will, when a man wills. The distance between "I can't" and "I did" is a long one, indeed. For only when there is "willing" is there a live possibility of "doing".

Self-discipline is the key which can make our will work for us. It can unlock the door which leads to our higher selves and train us in the ways of confidence.

In the past, traditional moral codes underscored the benefits that grew out of self-discipline. Today, the "modern" theme is "self-expression"! Do what you please, when you please, how you please! No inhibitions, please; no slavishness to silly ideals or foolish, high-minded goals.

The ancient world used the charioteer and his horses as an illuminating example. Locking up the horses in the stable, they called inhibition. Setting them loose, in order to run wild and menace people, was called self-expression. Harnessing them to a chariot—putting them to some useful, fruitful task—they knew as self-discipline. But "self-discipline" is out of style today. Most people are satisfied to hitch their star to a wagon and so they never hitch their wagon to a star! They "can't" because they "won't"!

"May Thy will become my will." So runs an ancient Hebrew prayer. But learning God's will cannot help the man who has none of his own!

YOUR SPIRITUAL RESOURCES ARE MANY

Even a mountain climber reaches a peak and can go no higher.

Swimmers and racers have their allotted margins of endurance—not to speak of man's machines, which burn out after whirring through their "lifespan". In the realm of the physical world we reach high points which prevent our going any further. We reach a state of exhaustion.

But it is not so with man's spirit:

We can wear our minds out in study, and there is always more mind with which to study.

We can give our heart in love, and yet there is always more heart with which to love.

When we show great compassion and pity, instead of becoming weak, we become very strong. The more we give of ourselves the more we have left to give.

Too many of us aim for milestones that turn out to be monumental dead ends. Sometimes we spend a whole lifetime just getting ready to set out for mountain tops of our desires. When we get there, we discover no place to go but down. This happens to people whose goals are purely material, for whom reality consists only of the tangible, the visible, the current, and the immediate goods of life.

How many lives have been wasted in the pursuit of unhappy happiness—in the quest for a joy that fades and jades, that flickers and dies?

Even our luxuries have their boundaries. A man cannot sleep on more than one bed at a time or drive two automobiles at once. Material possessions cannot buy love and sweet friendship. When you are all alone, you can't easily sit on top of the world.

The real satisfactions in life are those that touch the spiritual dimensions of man's being. There the questions are different: Not how much you have or what have you acquired—but how much have you given and what have you rejected. Not what you have desired, but what you have needed. Not the speed of your achievement, but the direction of your thought.

And most important: Not the mountains you have climbed, but how you have walked through the valley of shadows.

YOU CAN BEGIN AGAIN

Flaubert said genius is only long patience and hard work. Michelangelo is supposed to have said this:

"If people knew how hard I work to get my mastery, it wouldn't seem so unusual at all."

There is much that we can learn from these masters. Nothing significant comes easily. We purchase cheaply only the allurements of life.

How true this is of all our real and lasting treasures. Start with our home life. Some couples wrongly think love and family unity are possible without constant effort.

Bad coffee in the morning has been blamed sometimes for wrecked homes. A powder keg full of trivia, adding up to nothing, has blown up many a marriage.

But a good home, because it is the greatest work of art achievable by man, takes time and patience. We never can take love for granted.

We have to keep polishing our loyalty and our devotion to keep them from tarnishing. We have to work at being good husbands and wives, sincere fathers and mothers.

We never reach a stage of completion or perfection. We can't rest on our laurels.

The moment we think we've achieved complete and final understanding, we may be on our way to losing it. But fortunately for the rational man and woman, life affords many chances. If we've made mistakes—and who hasn't?—we always can try to rebuild the bridge. We can recapture love that has rusted by lack of use.

Our trouble is that we imagine the tasks and challenges of life so formidable we never make a real start at tackling them. Broken homes often are not so much broken as they are deserted. Deserted by people who refuse to expend the effort to solve their problems.

It's the first step that counts. Even a trip around the world begins by taking the first step. Once we're on the way, the road becomes easier and the direction clearer.

KNOW THYSELF!

The trees began to weep, the story goes, when they saw that iron had been created.

They feared the axes which would be made to destroy them. But a wise voice offered a consolation:

"Fear not, the iron cannot harm you unless you yourselves supply the wood for the axes' handles."

We have a carload of fears, many more of shadow than of substance. We forget today fretting about tomorrow. Frightened by our future, we try to revive ancient yesterdays. We live with nightmares instead of dreams.

We don't trust ourselves. We set up imaginary enemies and shoot our missiles in every direction, seeking to destroy the wrong foe. We rant against the fates and are drowned by our tears and fears. But the thing we fear most is our own self.

And this happens to people who really don't know themselves. They may be most proficient in many of the arts and sciences but they are utterly ignorant of who and what they themselves are.

We're often so busy getting and storing knowledge about the world that we neglect to get to know ourselves.

Limitation is the first guide to self-knowledge, as it is with all knowledge. Any student who thinks he knows all there is to know, knows very little indeed. You begin by recognizing the boundaries of your field.

You learn a good deal about what you can do, when you've discovered what you can't do.

And so with every man. Know your own borders, your own limits and limitations! Make peace with these and then take the next step—concentrate! The scientist who knows his field is the one who has concentrated upon it. He may be a poor philosopher but he can be a good biologist.

He knows his work best who knows the weakness, but also the greatness, of his borderline. It's what you do in the interior that helps defend the coast.

KNOW MORE THAN THYSELF!

Many things are not really what they seem. There is a kind of unreality even about the biggest things. Things that loom very big are really just a fraction of their seeming size. What seem to be mountains are really molehills.

And what is true of things is also true of ideas. We sometimes have big ideas about ourselves and other people that turn out to be Tom-Thumb thoughts.

Consider the people who are provincial and contrast them with those who call themselves cosmopolitan. What makes a man provincial or cosmopolitan has little to do with the place in which he lives. It is rather an attitude of the mind.

The cosmopolitan thinks of himself as urbane, but more often than not he is only urban, or perhaps suburban. In his desire to be "a citizen of the world", he belongs to nothing because he thinks that he belongs to everything. It turns out that the strangest kind of provincial is the cosmopolitan. He is often glib and is usually a dilettante who lacks convictions of his own.

He dresses up and covers himself with the quilted patchwork of other people's ideas, which he borrows for each special occasion.

Lessons from the lives of great men are available: Albert Schweitzer is a citizen of the world because, in a certain secluded spot in Africa, he reached the deepest meaning of life—of all life. And Gandhi and Weizmann were such people. Like Schweitzer, they had deep roots in their own tradition, a profound fervour and zeal.

But always they had the understanding that what they were doing was related to the deepest needs of all men.

"Deep calleth unto deep." To be sure, we have got to belong to something if anything is to belong to us. But always, if what we believe in belongs to us alone, we remain provincial despite our cosmopolitan claims.

When the boundaries of space or colour divide us from each other, we become less than what we were destined to be. If we know only ourselves, we really never get to be our best selves. There is one antidote to being either provincial or cosmopolitan. We need to be fully human.

We are less than human because instead of seeking to know our fellow men, we tend to fear those who are different from ourselves.

One wise grandfather played an instructive trick on his grandchildren. He pulled an imaginary pistol from his pocket and pointed his finger at them as if it were a gun. And then came his lesson.

"If I were a stranger in the dark", he explained, "and I pointed a gun at you, you would be frightened out of your wits.

But if you know me and you know that my weapon is a toy, you would just laugh it off.

"Fears", he suggested, "are just like that. If you understand what causes them, you become familiar with them; then you can easily get rid of them with a quick shrug and a calm smile."

He was right. We fear the things and the people we do not know.

One social scientist tested this proposition on students in eight different colleges. He listed forty-nine groups and asked students to indicate whether or not they would admit them to the country, grant them citizenship, give them employment, accept them as classmates, permit them to move next door, fraternize with them, and perhaps marry them.

Among the forty-nine groups, he listed the "Danireans", "Pireneans", and "Wallonians". None of the students could ever have met a Danirean, a Pirenean, or a Wallonian. As a matter of fact, no one has; these are names of non-existent people. But the study proved that students who revealed intolerance of other groups on the list, had similar attitudes towards these mythical, non-existent people.

We also fear ourselves and lack self-confidence for similar reasons. We are paralyzed by frights that are more imaginary than real. We have got to learn how to turn on the lights and smile calmly as the shadows disappear. And for every one of our real troubles, there is a latent power within us waiting to be known and used.

We are just not familiar with our best selves. We often do not know our own strength. When we are hurt by insensitivity or cruelty, our best weapon is kindness, for one who is compassionate cannot have his feelings hurt. When we are bowed with sorrow we find a cure through our sympathy and tenderness for the suffering of others.

Some of us are able to cram a lot of facts and figures into our heads, and we call this knowledge.   But there is no greater fact or figure than man and his fellow man.   We get to know ourselves by knowing our neighbours.   This is the most useful kind of knowledge we can ever acquire.

JUDGE THYSELF!

Are you one of the "S" men?   Beware, if you are, for you betray the signs of stunted spiritual growth.

They are three in kind, these "S" men who have just not grown up.   Each is the product of arrested emotional development.   And the pity—for none seems to know it.

The first is the "sneer".   He comes in two varieties.   He may be the successful man who misunderstands his success and believes he alone is responsible for it, he alone knows it all. He resembles the little boy who has mastered one of the multiplication tables, and then sits back and listens mockingly to the mistakes of others.   He is convinced nobody else can do it as well.

Or the other type of "sneer".   He has failed at so many things for lack of patience or stick-to-it-iveness that he can't understand the man who does succeed.   No man, he believes, is capable of achievement by virtue of his own mettle.   The successful man can only be the product of somebody's special influence.

The sneer, of either stripe, is looking always in the wrong direction.   He fails to take other people into account.   His gaze is tightly focused only on himself and he can't see the world around him.

He moves within the narrow circle of his own conceits or his own wounds and never reaches out to feel the heartbeat of his fellows. No man is a man who doesn't feel for other men. He's an emotional baby, instead!

And the "snob". He, too, is a spiritual dwarf. He is certain that a natural and obvious gulf divides him from most people. While he may believe in the proposition that all men are created equal, he is certain he is "more equal" than all the others. He lives as though he was perpetually saying:

"There is no need for me to know what you know; no need for you to know what I know. After all we are so different from each other."

His arrogance, however, really betrays his insecurity, his immaturity. He is not a "grown up" because he has "grown in".

The "sniper" completes our roster of "S" men. He's always shooting from ambush because he's certain everyone's shooting at him. He can always explain or rationalize his own shortcomings. But not those of the other man—the other fellow is always to blame.

So he's prepared to go through life criticizing, hurting, and destroying other people with or without provocation. He believes, it seems, in "preventive wars". Beat down the world before it does the same to you!

The sneer, the snob, and the sniper may be big in their own eyes, and even in the eyes of those who behold them. For all that, they are little indeed, spiritually undersized—men who fall short of real manhood.

They judge everyone but themselves. Their apparent superiority feelings are only a cloak for their basic lack of self-confidence; whereas, the confident man can look into his mirror and honestly judge himself.

DON'T BE BORED!

Recently a doctor said:

"The most deadly disease from which people are suffering today is one that medicine cannot reach.   It cannot be cured by the surgeon's knife."

Someone asked if he was referring to cancer.

He replied:

"No, we are on the track of cancer, and sooner or later we will find its causes and cures.   The disease I refer to is boredom."

How right he is!   Have you ever noticed how many of your friends and acquaintances literally are "bored to death"?   Strange irony.   While science is helping man win the fight for a longer existence, countless thousands are losing the battle for life. And principally because they know so little about their inner, spiritual powers.   If they knew themselves aright, they could easily wage and win a preventive war against this menacing human blight.

Many of us are "bored to death" because, living only for ourselves, we are "dead to the world".   We live in cramped quarters.   We dwell in valleys and do not lift up our eyes to the mountains.

We are not bored as a result of the things we have, but because of the things we do not have—the faith that prolongs our lives into eternity, and the view that links us to the world around us.

The human being needs altitude.   He requires hopes that soar far beyond personal interest and practical need.

Boredom is easy for the selfish, difficult for the selfless. Whenever you see a man filled with the fire of life, you know that there are purposes on his horizon which go far beyond mere self-satisfactions.

The difference between enthusiasm and boredom is often the difference between a man who has learned how to jump out of his own skin and one who is intent only upon saving it.

And life also becomes monotonous when we drain ourselves dry of its drama. We were made for growth. We begin dying when we stop growing and permit our hearts and minds to lie fallow.

We ought to remember that no man ever was born great. Moses, the Bible suggests, "grew up" into greatness.

This can happen to us—but only when instead of shrinking we expand and grow greatly. Consider the people of fifty years of age who pine over their lost youth, forgetting that only age can bring the depth, wisdom, and insight which are the ingredients of real happiness.

Instead of wallowing in self-pity, crying over the dreams we have not fulfilled, when we reach advanced years, we can find meaning in the visions of others, gaining strength and joy from the immortal vigour of ideas.

What is more: As we grow older, if we are truly mature, we will want to be what we are, for we'll have known what it has meant to be young when we were young. Instead of seeking happiness in trying to recapture something we have lost, we can still learn how to be ourselves and yet enjoy it.

When youthful zest gives way to the grey hairs of age, for those who have truly been young, there is still much that can be done and will be done. For dreams do not die, even though dreamers must.

And the knowledge garnered over the years can teach us how to transform vapid vision into living reality. Something of heaven, when young hearts are supported by wise heads, can be brought down to earth.

SEEK ADVENTURE

Suppose you tell a man a story of great adventure—how a friend walked one day in a forest, lost his way, and then waited for nightfall to make flares to light up the sky.

You describe two days and two nights of loneliness, of terror and fear. Finally, you dramatize the escape. Your friend is sighted by a helicopter, which seeks a clearing, lands, and brings him back alive. And after this hair-raising story, the man who has been listening all the while without a display of emotion, says:

"There's nothing so unusual about that!"

This man, like many others, is a "so-what-er"—a person who has lost his sense of thrill, of wonder and surprise. No matter what great or thrilling thing happens, his major reaction is one of "so what!"

The pity of this is that it can happen to anybody. But the striking fact is that the older we get, the more we are subject to the disease of "so-what-itis".

It is, unhappily, a contagious, communicable disease. If we consort with people who are afflicted by it, we may very well catch it. Yet, there are many cases on record that prove it is a curable malady. One therapy consists of a very simple procedure: Just take a walk under the canopy of the skies, making certain all the time to get the fog out of your eyes so that you can see clearly what is really before you.

Unfortunately, there are cases which indicate that some people cannot see the forest because of the trees. Strange to say, there are many people like this—people who get up every morning, dress hurriedly, eat the same breakfast, rush off to work, see the same people, do the same things, and never are aware of the world of beauty that immediately surrounds them.

In the Bible we have the record of a man of a different stripe. He said:

"The heavens declare the glory of God, and the firmament shows His handiwork. Day unto day expresses His greatness, night unto night makes Him known."

This man knew the beauty and the revival of life, because he knew and was close to the whole world of nature.

But talk to a man who is a prisoner of canyons of steel and stone about some of these things. His answers are of utter emptiness, an emptiness that echoes the hollowness within him. He has lost his sense of wonder and surprise because he is out of touch with God's world and only in touch with his own.

Young people have a lot to teach their elders. More than their elders realize. They still have a sense of excitement in their doing, because they are filled with the joy of being alive and with the romance of growing and aspiring.

But youth is an attitude of mind as well as a time of life. People grow older. But sometimes they grow down and not up. Growing up means holding on to and keeping alive the spirit of adventure and the thrill of living.

As long as you can still be amazed to your very core over the wonderful simplicities of God's world, you are young despite your years.

The adventurous soul knows how to seek out new reasons for joy in living. The search itself is the adventure. And the sense of gratitude which follows is the fibre which encloses the deeper fulfillments of our spirit.

AVOID EXCESSES

"Too little" is the twin of "too much". Those who have too little self-confidence often betray their lack, by too much talking, too much pushing, too much bragging. Three kinds of people would do well to underplay their overdone, frenetic zeal.

The first of the trio may be conveniently dubbed as Mr. Over-Aggressive. We find him everywhere we go. He's forever fussing, feuding, and fuming.

His shirts are never laundered right; his coffee's never hot enough. He vows vengeance on the whole dry-cleaning industry and upon all of the world's poor and unsuspecting waiters. He makes the mistake of assuming that he has been made the special, supreme target of all assorted inadequacies. For, after all, he tells himself, the earth and the fulness thereof are his.

His life is eloquent testimony to stored-up aggressions which he makes no attempt to control, subdue, or sublimate. He has never learned to be still and contemplate, to think rather than grunt. He might live longer himself if he were willing to let others live longer.

The over-competitive man is our next victim of excess. Competition, of itself, need not destroy our values or our hearts. If it is not the total measure of our life's work, competition can spur us without injury. But success comes to those who learn how to work with people, not against them; when we are consumed with a passion to win all the time, we must slowly go down the road to self-destruction.

The over-competitive man harbours jealousy and hate, which is the double product of the resentment of others. He believes that he can achieve victory only when the other fellow loses. But life is filled with victories which are really defeats, and losses which may become gains.

If we refuse to co-operate with life's inexorable logic and unnecessarily insist upon competing all the time, we have lost the race long before it begins.

The third victim of immaturity is the man who never grows up—he thinks that the only way to remain active is to be over-active. And so, he is constantly running, proving himself, and impressing others with his strength and prowess. But to grow old is not a sin; it is an art.

There comes a time in life when we need no longer behave like children in order to prove how youthful we are. One of the signs of immature youth is its consistent insistence upon action for action's sake.

Maturity knows what not to do; it has already outgrown the stage of frenetic doing and is quite prepared to let the more foolish burn out their physical machines in exciting but empty whirligigging. Wise men are active but not frantic.

To those who would shed their insecurities: Stop being over-aggressive, over-competitive, over-active! The confident soul is quiet, noiseless. It learns to avoid excesses.

BE BETTER THAN AVERAGE

Character and culture—two key words that tell an important tale.

There is a road leading through Binghamton, New York, that bears two numbers: Routes 11 and 17. For seven miles Routes 11 and 17 are one and the same road. But suddenly there comes a fork.

Route 11 turns right, into Pennsylvania, and Route 17 veers left, continuing in New York State. One leads into flat plains; the other, into rolling, hilly countryside.

These roads are like life itself. There are many important moments when the roads seem to be the same—when people seem to be very much like one another, and yet, they are so different. This is what we mean when we speak of "character". Our own habits and attitudes make us into unique beings, each with his own wants and needs, his dreams and hopes.

But at the side of character there is something man calls culture. Despite our differences, our roads often converge. The society in which we live, the customs, manners, and behaviour patterns—the culture of which we are a part—very often puts us all together, on the same road.

In common, we of our culture share the anxieties caused by problems of war and peace. In common, we share both the blessings and the tensions born of an industrial setting, where production is king.

There are, however, a limited number of people in every walk of life who are so constituted that they are willing to do—indeed, eager to do—more than their duty. There is a feeling of specialness about such people. Theirs are lives which are filled with extra touches.

There is something within that moves us when we meet such people. I remember being taught the story of Cain and Abel as a child. On the face of it, we children could not understand why it was that God favoured the offering of Abel over the offering of Cain—the text itself is silent on the question.

It was only when our teacher explained that Cain had brought only what he had been asked to bring, while Abel did more than he was asked, that the story took on special meaning.

Or, we remember the story of Abraham—how, when strangers appeared near his tent, he ran forward to greet them and willingly offered them the hospitality of his humble dwelling.

What remains with us of that story is "the extra touch" of hospitality which Abraham displayed. He not only put up the strangers and cared for them and their animals; he went out of his way, running down the road, to make certain that he would personally greet them.

Each of us possesses two potentialities. We can be just like everyone else. Or, we may be different, special, unique. Our man-made culture makes us quite like the next fellow. It is our character that gives us a chance to be more than ordinary.

Sometimes we are only a reflection of the world around us. No worse, but no better. Other times we show the capacity to move upward, to let our character shine through. When that happens, we tread roads that lift us into new realms and heights.

The confident person is the one whose strength of character gains continuing victories over the powerful onslaughts of an overbearing culture.

Prophets come close to having a perfect score. We cannot all be prophets. But, by improving our "average", we can become better than average. And that is the proper use of character.

LEARN HOW TO STAY YOUNG

"It takes pounds off your waist and years off your face."

Any such advertisement is, quite likely to sell its wares successfully anywhere in the land. One of the most common traits of our countrymen is their desire to look and feel younger than they are. And it is a good characteristic. It is a hopeful sign of vitality and renewal.

But the methods used to achieve this goal are based upon a misunderstanding. Most people don't realize that this question is tied up more with their spiritual than with their physical structure. To look young we must never succumb to cynicism. Cynicism is a morbid distrust of anyone but ourselves, and it can cause more psychological grey hair than a hornet's nest of troubles.

There are many people who won't trust themselves and who need constant reassuring and propping. This is an ailment of immaturity. But one of the maladies that sometimes accompanies "maturity" is the ugly and frightened kind of thing that makes us sceptical and suspicious of the intentions of everyone around us.

The scoffing cynic betrays his lack of faith. And this is what makes him old, long before his time. What is more, he stubbornly stands as an obstacle to growth and development. He is a symbol of sickening decay who can only invoke the "good old times".

The moment a man starts glorifying the good old times and can only be critical of the present, he betrays his lack of faith as well as his spiritual age.

Many a father has impeded his children by not knowing how to let go of the reins to permit these young lives to test their own sprouting wings. This kind of distrust breeds contempt and only widens the chasm between the generations.

And many a wholesome community institution, church, or club has lost its mission and vitality because elders destroyed a living faith, by their suspicions of youth and their lack of confidence in them. Scores of promising groups have forfeited their usefulness because of this kind of spiritual rigor mortis.

When new ideas are blocked by our obstinate heads, for fear that we may be overtaken and replaced by younger people, we have grown very old indeed.

Do you want to know how to keep young? Accept young people, encourage them, trust them. Above all, be with them! The Scout leader, the community club worker, the church leader, and the Sunday school teacher have a long lease on youthfulness because they serve and do not fear young people.

The next time you find yourself laughing at young people, stop in your tracks, and try laughing with them.

LEARN HOW TO LAUGH

There are times when we need a sense of humour more than anything else. Having it and using it can change our lives.

Ironically, the man who lacks this sixth sense easily can make a fool of himself. He makes mountains of molehills and is tyrannized by trivia.

A man and wife were quarrelling bitterly. Her pride was hurt and she shouted through her tears. His manliness was wounded and he raged with the roar of lions. Suddenly their son, aged five, entered the room. In his hand he carried a large hair brush. He fixed his reproving eyes on them both. There was a long, hushed minute of silence. Then came the challenge, sweetly lisped:

"I don't know which one needs to be spanked!"

Shamed, the boy's parents broke into laughter. Within a few minutes, they saw how ridiculous was their recent storm.

A good deal of the time our petty annoyances mount to gigantic disturbances because we take ourselves too seriously. At others we'll laugh, expecting them to laugh with and not at us. But he only is not laughed at who learns to laugh at himself first.

Trees that never bend fall mightily.   And sometimes at the slightest gusts.

So it is with rigid and stiff stuffed-shirts of men.   They may strut pompously, but they stand precariously.   They walk with heads so high in the clouds that their two feet are no longer on the ground.   They may be great scientists, philosophers, or businessmen — but they've lost vital, vibrant contact with people.

We know that infants respond to smiling affection with a spontaneous glow of love.   By nature, then, we've got all it takes to be sunny and happy.   But as we go through life, we sometimes learn bad habits that make us windier and more blustery than we were meant to be.

We blow when we should glow.   We howl when we should smile.   We take ourselves seriously when we should be laughing at our foibles.

And it is simpler than we think to be happy and well-adjusted.   Look in the mirror.   If people don't warm up to you easily, it may be because you've forgotten how to smile. Unknown to you, they may be frightened by the impression of your expression.

A smiling face rarely fails to penetrate even the coldest, iciest hearts.   Inbuilt radiant heat is the best social anti-freeze available.   It provides the simple warmth so necessary for an attractive, confident personality.

To know how and when to smile or laugh is a great blessing. Good humour can be a simple therapy for some of our home-grown ills.   It not only relaxes our muscles, it also can untie some of our spiritual knots.

Life is a serious business, but it need not be humourless. Therefore, beware the man who treats the insignificant and the important with equal gravity.   He is as poorly oriented to life as one who treats these with equal levity.

The proverb sums it up: He who is always laughing is a fool; and he who never laughs is a knave.

But always there comes pity for the fellow whose self-centredness and lack of self-confidence blinds him from the wisdom of life. He cuts himself down by his own hand. Instead of knowing how to smile little things away, internal combustion makes him explode.

Truly, he who laughs, lasts.

LEARN HOW TO PLAY

A psychiatrist says: "Many people haven't any real, specific problems—except the general problem of themselves. They'd be all right if they would just stop fuming and fretting about themselves and everything in general."

For some of us, most of our problems would find solution if we would only learn how to quiet down. But how do you do that in a mad world?

The first requirement is to reduce our pace, or at least the tempo of our race. We literally cut ourselves to shreds with our own hands. We permit ourselves to become over-stimulated, over-excited; we run in many directions at once.

Much of today's "recreation", it has been properly said, must be spelled w-r-e-c-k-reation. People who live hard and work hard think they also have to play hard. The result is self-indulgence requiring vacations from vacations.

Relaxation, one of the gods of an over-industrialized personality, is thought to be the result of "a change of pace" from normal, fatiguing routines; it is not yet linked to a reduction of pace. Actually, the tempo of our lives has more to do with our unhappiness than most realize. We are confused because we are bored; bored because we are tired; tired because we are running all the time.

To relax is to allow oneself a healthy indifference to things that really don't matter; to look at this moment, this hour, with the emotional apathy that realizes that there will be other moments, other hours. Not all was made to be achieved at once; not every flower is a perennial, many are annuals. Even God Himself did not finish the work of Creation; He left much for man to achieve with Him and for Him!

Relaxation is not the product of inertia, lack of concern, or dullness of spirit. Indeed, it is rooted in moods and feelings which are the obverse of these. It weighs and measures significances; it stores up emphatic energies for moments that need them. It helps us not to spend our strength too democratically; not to labour mightily over molehills, when we should be conserving our power to scale mountains.

The race, we have been taught, is not to the swift. But we are victims of the false belief that we've got to run in order to win. One teacher taught: "Whatever it is we want, it will be there when we get there. If it is not there—it was not supposed to be there. If we miss it, perhaps we should have missed it. If we miss it, we will never know whether we would have liked it or not!"

Certainly we need to learn how to play. Dr. Karl A. Menninger, the famous psychiatrist, was surely right when he wrote: "People who don't play are potentially dangerous. There seems to be a general idea that recreation is all right if one does not take it too seriously. My belief is that much the greater danger lies in not taking it seriously enough."

To stop fuming and fretting so much, we need to seek the spiritual pauses that refresh, to stop wanting so many inappropriate things, that keep us from appreciating what we already have. Confidence depends upon quiet and grateful hearts.

LEARN HOW TO LOVE

We can endure a wide variety of discomfort. We withstand poverty and the perils of physical danger. Yet, life seems to run out into the depths if deep down within us there is a gnawing sense of loneliness.

As children we exhibit the fears of abandonment. We crave the light, shun the darkness. We are comforted when we are certain that a beloved is close at hand. No matter how old or grey we grow, we never outgrow the heart's craving for the understanding and sympathy of someone who cares. We never move beyond the need for the wisdom of Genesis: "It is not good for man to be alone." Indeed, at the very heart of all human bereavement are the aches and pains of loneliness, the forlorn feelings of having been utterly and finally abandoned.

Is there no answer, no therapy for our ills? Are there no ways in which we may fortify our lives against that dark feeling of being adrift on a wide sea, with no one to hold our hand? There are.

First, we ought to understand what causes loneliness. People are lonely because they run away from unpleasant reality. We wish to have limitless pleasure and, often, are unwilling or unable to endure its absence. We cringe before the demands life makes of us. We close our eyes to the sordid, the difficult, and the tormenting.

The tragedy of loneliness finds its effective answer in a single word: Love.

But what kind of love? Not the love which is given in order to receive. For if love is only given to be received, when we no longer receive it, we are left all alone, profoundly troubled and unhappy, believing that we have been rejected. Love must be a free gift; it must be given as a supreme act of faith. What is more: It must reflect a confident affirmation of life. Real love says: In spite of my own hurt, I want to help things grow; I want to help the seed take root; I want to see life aspire and achieve. And it says one thing more: "I will labour that life may grow."

This kind of love reflects our embrace of the fullness of life.

He who loves in this mature way will never really feel rejected by life.

Part IV

HAVE

CONFIDENCE

IN OTHERS

A. UNDERSTAND CONFIDENCE

CONFIDENCE IS BASED UPON TRUTH

"What Peter says about Paul tells you more about Peter than about Paul."

That was this man's way of reacting to those whose gossip assailed his ears.

He was a good man. "But I am always afraid of being so good", he would say, "that I might become a menace."

"A menace?" we asked in amazement. "Yes, a menace. You see, too many good people teach themselves to believe that all's right with the world, and they couldn't possibly be the cause of what might go wrong anyway. They always have someone else handy, to blame."

"Whenever anybody comes to me and says: 'Did you hear what everybody's saying about so and so?' I answer him with my own question. 'Who is saying it?' I ask. 'Everybody, or just you?' Most gossips are such frightened little cowards. They try to sell as unadulterated truth what in fact are only their own small personal prejudices."

We sat and talked and I felt the impact of a good man who was willing to work at being good. He continued talking. "Habitual gossipers are a dime a dozen. They take over the conversation at dinner tables, card tables, and assorted parties. Wherever there is small talk, the gossiper is in the saddle. And because most of us, these days, have very little to say, we begin to talk about people rather than to people. But really, it's not the gossiper who is to blame."

"Who is?" we queried. Without blinking an eye, he parried: "Why, it's the fellow who is willing to listen to the nonsense. He's the one who actually commits the gravest error. That's what I mean by the 'menace' of good people. They never say a bad word about anybody, but they encourage others to do so when they don't stop them."

Then, to cap the conversation, he referred to a Hebrew proverb. "What people forget", he suggested, "is that death and life are in the hands of the tongue."

One wonders how much we recognize the truth of that statement. Words once uttered carry with them grave responsibility. What we say about people may not only destroy them, but can destroy us in the process.

The witch-hunts of Salem, Massachusetts, are an eloquent reminder of how much our lives depend upon the truth of what we say. There, an entire community was on the verge of self-destruction because it accepted as fact the gossip of fools and children.

Well enough for an ivory-tower philospher to proclaim: " 'They say'. What do they say? Let them say!" Good and sufficient for the mountain dweller, for him who lives in rarefied, remote atmosphere. No such philosophical aloofness can help us ordinary mortals. We are all involved in the life of the other. What "they say" does and should matter to us. For "they say" may soon become "we say" and before long all of us may be infected with distrust of each other. What starts as a minor illness may become epidemic.

There can be no family life, no economy, no political freedom, no international harmony without confidence. And there is no confidence that is not firmly based upon truth and the reverence of truth. Sooner or later truth catches up with slander; but sometimes it is too late: hope may be lost, lives destroyed, freedom defeated.

Good families and good communities stand by Paul until they're certain of Peter. If they let Peter wag his tongue easily, what Peter says about Paul may one day destroy them, too.

CONFIDENCE IS ROOTED
IN TRUE EDUCATION

Now that sputniks and luniks are whirling high above us, the "egghead" has come back into fashion and is again in society's good graces. But scant years ago, intellectuals were in disrepute; anyone with a college education was suspected of being "too smart for his own good".

But the pendulum which swings too rapidly sometimes gets stuck at one extreme after the other. For now, there is great commotion and combustion—something resembling scrambled egg-heads. Education is vital to the survival of the West, we are now told; without a stepping-up of our brain power, we may face total blackout.

So far so good. But what kind of education? Is "education for survival" merely to be concerned with science and technology, with rocketry and space magic? Or do we need now, as never before, to create not just "tinkering men", but thinking men, as well?

Education is life, and there is more to life than physical excellence. True education involves an awareness of the need to cultivate the heart as well as the mind. Nor is it confined to the single subject matter of religion or morals. Broadly conceived, it is a mood which must permeate everything that is taught. A good clue to what is required is found in the recorded conversations of the principal of an English college and a schoolmaster. Inquired the former of the latter: "Where in your timetable do you teach religion?"

"We teach it all day long", replied the teacher. "We teach it in arithmetic by accuracy. We teach it in language by learning to say what we mean. We teach it in history by humanity. We teach it in geography by breadth of mind. We teach it in handicraft by thoroughness. We teach it in astronomy by reverence. We teach it in the playground by fair play. We teach it by courtesy to servants, by good manners to one another, and by truthfulness in all things. We teach it by showing the children that we, their elders, are their friends and not their enemies."

There you have it. Subject matter matters, but it is not the heart of the matter. Our schools need to teach the three R's and much more. But teachers must remember that they are teaching children, not arithmetic. They must impart knowledge, but more important, they need to inspire hearts and elevate minds.

When scientists discovered electricity there could have been eternal cause for joy and rejoicing. Nobody, at that time, identified electricity with death in the electric chair.

Look at our world now. Every time we consider the words "atomic energy", instead of being gladdened and strengthened by it, we fearfully think of missiles, rockets, bombs, and sputniks.

Again one thinks of the phrase from the Psalmist: "Passing through the valley of weeping they yet make it a place of springs." Not what we meet in life, but what we do with what we meet; not the ordeals and the sacrifices, but what we make of our trials, is the key to the meaning of our universal pain.

Suffer, sacrifice, we must. But what will we do with the lessons of our suffering? Will we learn to make it serve a purpose, not destructive and not disastrous?

Education which is geared to moral values, which teaches us to view life as a spiritual adventure is the need of the hour. We have too long believed that human confidence grows out of the physical skills and mechanical techniques which we have learned in our scientifically oriented classrooms. The truth lies in the opposite direction. Far from gaining real confidence from technology, we are literally scared to death by what our "educated" minds are now capable of achieving. To gain real confidence, we need to seek the education of our hearts; we need to become proficient in the art of living more than in the technology of death.

Humpty-Dumpty, we need remember, had a great fall. That is because he was more egg than man, more head than heart. We need to be put together again. Our heads and our hearts need to be synchronized in a new harmony which will keep the moon safe, not only for experiments but also for light—and even for love.

CONFIDENCE COMES FROM COMMITMENT

We sat and talked about serious things, ultimate things. There were thirty of us, and each man was asked to tell what he "wanted out of life".

As each rose to report his hopes and to share his dreams, a connecting thread was woven between all. Their desires seemed to be of the very same cloth. Over and over we heard the same words: health, happiness, security, peace of mind.

And then suddenly the discussion moved to a different level, a level these busy businessmen had somehow forgotten.

Someone said:

"Isn't it strange that all of us are speaking the same language; we're talking of the pursuit of personal happiness as our major goal, and yet even as we speak these words, we are conscious that there must be more to living than just this.

"Perhaps the reason we are giving these strange answers is that we are asking the wrong questions."

"How would you put the questions?" shot back one man.

"I'll tell you", the first answered. "It is not so important ot ask 'what do I want out of life' as it is to know what life wants out of me!"

And then he went on to explain his position. The Greeks, he said, were the inventors of the philosophy of "eat, drink, and be merry". This was, and is, the attitude which believes that what's good for me is good for the world.

But the ancient Hebrew prophets looked at life differently. They put the equation the other way: what's good for the world, what's good for the community of men, should be good for me, too.

Micah, the speaker reminded them, formulated this position in a classical way. The prophet asked his people:

"What doth the Lord require of thee?" He didn't say: "What do you require of the Lord?"

When we go around seeking only the fulfillment of our personal amibitions, we end up in frustration and often in despair. When we go about life asking ourselves what our duties are, what our commitments must be, we develop a way of living which gives us buoyancy and inner strength.

We can never be satisfied with ourselves because we know that we need more than ourselves. There is too much in the life of others upon which we depend.

Atlas, the speaker concluded, was permitted the opinion that he was at liberty, if he wished, to drop the earth and creep away. But this opinion was all that he was permitted.

And so with all of us. We think that we can seek our own fulfillment without regard to our responsibilities to others. But this is only a wishful notion. If we drop our commitments and run away, we may think that we have achieved happiness or peace of mind. In reality we are left with nothing: everyone else will desert us, too.

Without a deep sense of commitment and a keen understanding of our duties to the world around us, we wouldn't be able to depend upon anyone. For our personal confidence is a function of the relationships we share with others.

If we are dependable, others will be. If we can trust in others, others can trust in us.

CONFIDENCE GROWS
WITH HONEST LIVING

Probe deeply into the nature of family and community life in our society and you will discover that one of the principal causes of uneasiness is an ethical difficulty arising out of faithlessness.

Parents often blindly utilize their authority in the name of of justice when they themselves act unjustly.

Faced with rebelliousness in their children, they shield themselves. But the law of justice operates without favouritism. If we have dealt dishonestly with our children, if we have told them that we are what we are not, if we preach to them without practising, we shall not pass the test of their rebellion.

We cannot, as parents, condone in ourselves what we condemn in our children.

Some of us view the rocking and rolling youngsters in our midst with jaundiced eyes. We question their new-fangled fads, their strange, sometimes raucous, behaviour, and wonder about their sense of balance. "This generation!" we sigh. "Where is it heading to?"

Well, who created this generation? And what do the antics of our children reflect? Expose young people to an atmosphere of idealism and see what happens! Give them a single standard of behaviour—one that applies to the parents as well—and observe the beneficial consequences.

We are also tested as husbands and wives by problems which are not so much psychological as religious. We cannot possibly emerge with clean hands, when we are unwilling to demand equally of ourselves what we insist upon in our beloved. When we speak of "faithfulness" in married life, we are really discussing a spiritual quality—not physical behaviour alone.

True faithfulness in our own private worlds requires that we be prepared to do what we ask others to do; to live by a single moral code in which we judge ourselves before we criticize others.

And so with the destiny of communities and nations. Democracy is now being tested in the very scales of this balance. Will there be freedom for all; or will there be freedom for only some? Will we meet the test of ruthless Soviet communism simply by criticizing that system, or by refining democracy?

Our society must constantly seek self-correction; blaming the evils of the world only upon others, makes us blind to the ethical decisions with which we are faced.

Recall the story of Abraham and Isaac. The patriarch is asked to sacrifice his only son. Had Abraham argued with God in order to save the life of his son, had he been critical and rebelled against the Divine command, the story might have ended differently. Isaac most probably would have been sacrificed after all: for Abraham would have missed the ethical issue at stake.

It was not the sacrifice of Isaac that God wanted; it was the devotion and the faith of Abraham!

An old Hebrew adage has it that "God sends a remedy to the world even before He sends the disease." On every front we are tested. Do we recognize the remedy and learn how to apply it; or are we so busy cursing the disease that we lose sight of the power we possess to overcome it?

As parents, as husbands and wives, and as nations, the problems we face are essentially ethical and spiritual. Are we prepared to live honestly by the light of our truest beliefs? If we are able to do this, we reflect the moral power that grows within us as we confidently face life.

CONFIDENCE SCORNS FALSE PRIDE

Pride destroys even the strongest.

They tell of a man who starved to death in a small town. He hid his plight from his neighbours. When the mayor heard of the tragedy, he said:

"That poor man did not die of hunger. He died of pride!"

There is hardly a man who hasn't been victimized, hurt by his own proud ego. Consider a few case histories:

Here's a man who tells you of his domestic problems: He's all riled up; his wife is not the woman he thought he married. She's critical, sensitive, spiteful. You ask if he's easy to get along with. And you often get an answer that goes like this:

"No, to tell the truth, I'm not an angel.   I've got my bad points, too.   Don't get me wrong, my wife has many, many fine qualities.   But—"

You suggest that he might tell his wife of her good points; and then you proceed calmly to discuss the exact irritants that are bothering him.   But enter pride and the remedy is foiled. He's boiling now, stirred by the hot fuel of an inflamed ego:

"After what she's said to me, I wouldn't give her such satisfaction."

Think of two neighbours.   They haven't talked to each other for ten years.   By now they can't remember the real cause of their estrangement.   Nevertheless, neither will be the first to say "good morning".   It would be a very simple thing, and really both are aching to do so.   But pride comes along again and erects a curtain between two families living side by side.

And the father who has destroyed the ties that bind the life of a child to a parent.   He knows that he's been too severe in the way he has judged his son.

False, bedevilling pride is keeping this father from doing what he knows is right.   He is frozen in his tracks, and the cold war goes on.

We've enough troubles to handle, enough sorrow and tragedy that torment us.   So pity the poor husband, the neighbour, and the father whose pride confounds their confusion, adding woes upon woes.   For their pride consumes them, destroys them.   They think that they are keeping their dignity and maintaining their postion.

But dignity and position are not protected by stiff necks and hard heads.   Only by warm and generous hearts.

Secure people do not make foolish pride into a substitute for the real dignity—the inner confidence which scorns false pride.

CONFIDENCE DEMANDS
RESPECT FOR OTHERS

Anyone knows that in the deepest sense all people are alike. What concerns us is that too few realize how much each group, although having a culture of its own, is a part of the common culture.

The rabbis of old once taught:

"If a man strikes many coins from one mold, they all resemble one another, but the King of Kings, the Holy One—blessed be He—fashioned every man in the stamp of the first man, and yet not one of them resembles his fellow. Therefore, every single person is obliged to say: 'The world was created for my sake.' "

The lesson is clear. When we recognize that each man is a distinct personality, possessing a self that is his very own, we understand more poignantly than ever that each possesses a uniqueness, and that this is equally true of the group, and of the faith group.

Each has something precious it wants to do and to say, to think and to believe. Each is struck from the same mold, and yet each is different.

The story of Creation possesses a profoundly simple "moral punch-line" which we regularly neglect. One man, we are reminded, was created—only one man! All other creatures were created according to their species—but only one man. The Bible is magnificently silent on the very subjects we moderns seem to say much about. It says nothing about the colour of Adam's skin, the speech of his tongue, or the creed of his heart.

Adam is the single father of humanity. No man may say: My father's people, my father's God was better than yours.

And yet a paradox hovers about us. If there is one human race, why, then, so many cultures, religions, and ways of life? One mankind, yes; but a variety of languages, ideas, lines of thought, national characters. This, too, is the work of God.

Many faiths, many peoples—each searching for a warm and pleasant place in the sun—do not destroy the unity of mankind, but, rather, reinforce it!

Sociologists, psychologists, historians, and others who proclaim these truths only remind us how small is the distance we have travelled since the Bible first taught the rule: Unity of mankind does not require uniformity of belief, culture, or national habit.

To understand this truly, we must avoid the glibness of extremism in our thinking. We have got to discard the naive view which recognizes that all men are equal and yet sees no meaning in any of their differences.

The differences of the various groups and religions have helped to challenge men's minds and souls. These differences have stimulated the advance of thought and the rise of civilization. Truly, without them, there would be no meaning to the similarities.

But we must also steer clear of jumping to the inane conclusion that, although all men are equal, our own group is "more equal" than any other. We are all commanded to "love thy neighbour as thyself". Add to love, knowledge and understanding, and see how the commandment reads.

If we know and understand our neighbours, we also get to know and understand ourselves. The man who knows only his own code, his own group, his own faith, does not really know even these.

The man who sees nothing of value in the tradition of others, probably has not penetrated the highest teachings and insights of his own tradition.

Rabbi Hillel once said:

"If I am not for myself, who will be for me; but if I am only for myself, what am I?"

For Jews, Catholics, and Protestants to achieve a confident and secure life of their own, this is the spirit in which they must approach the sacred lives of one another.

CONFIDENCE USES SETBACKS AS STEPPING STONES

The Hebrew Bible is a collection of narratives which depict the history of the Israelites, the birth and aspirations of a nation. Yet, the incidents which comprise this history concern living and vital people. What is more, the stories are told in a refreshingly relevant way: There is a mood of immediacy about them.

Such a story is the saga of Joseph. Joseph becomes, for the Biblical Author, a symbol of universal man: strong yet weak; passionate but flaccid; possessed by love, yet tormented by petty and childish grievances.

It is a remarkable story. Joseph first flits across the Biblical landscape as a starry-eyed youth, blighted by over-ambition; there is something of the "spoiled brat" about him.

His life unfolds before us in a series of events which open our eyes to the panorama of a man's character: how it is formed; how it grows up; how it is tested. The arrogant Joseph is repaid in kind by his brothers; they sell him as a slave.

But something happens to Joseph when he lands in Egypt. At every turn he is tested anew, and at every turn he withstands temptation. Finally, his brothers face him once more. He breaks down, backslides; the all-too-human desire for retaliation asserts itself. He taunts, cajoles, beguiles, and tantalizes them. He has his innings.

Joseph could not forget, and as long as he remained emotionally immature, he could not forgive, either. Then, suddenly, as in a storm, there came an unforgettable emotional experience in his life: all at once he grew up.

He has had his fun; at last he becomes the man! The mature Joseph shines through the blustering youth. He breaks down, reveals himself as their brother; therein is found the moral punch-line of the story.

He has had his opportunity to strike back at them for all of the childish wrongs they had inflicted upon him in his youth. But suddenly he becomes aware of his own childishness. Now that he has had his play, a mood of forgiveness floods him; he is emancipated from the juvenile spirit of vengeance. He becomes a mature person.

Joseph began as a child, but ended as a man. How many of us ever really become men?

Joseph arrived at the point of maturity out of an unlovely childhood. He dropped the old feuds and the immature grudges. How many of us learn how to forgive and forget?

Win or lose, we often act as if "the fight must go on." Many of us do not even realize that we maintain our battle positions long after the struggle has been lost.

Joseph became a man when he became a brother. Joseph the slave hated: Joseph the Viceroy of Egypt forgave. As we develop inner security, we no longer need to hate. As we grow emotionally tall, we feel safe; we trust ourselves to ourselves! We can grow without seeking our neighbour's destruction!

CONFIDENCE FACES LIFE
REALISTICALLY

"I want and need peace of mind."

The man who said that to me was probably repeating what millions of others said or felt that very moment. For some it was an expression of a need to face more heroically a death or a tragedy that had come upon them. Others were plagued and obsessed by money matters or job insecurity. But for many the phrase came as a deep sigh over trivia that may have been disturbing, but should not have been distressing.

I knew someone who could help this man, and so we went to visit my friend, who was grey with age and insight. We found him, as usual, sitting in a seaside park, looking at the great world about him and learning from it. All around us, there were men with worried faces, each bearing some inner burden.

We three walked along silently, my friend puffing softly on his pipe. Soon he stopped and pointed to a tree. He said: "This tree—here is a sermon in God's language. Leafy branches, soaring limbs—but look better at its roots. We have wisdom without deeds, minds without hearts. But noble thought without noble action is like a rootless tree—it cannot long endure. Life is too short to be little", he said.

"We need big hearts for big deeds, even in little things." And looking up to the horizon, he uttered an unforgettable thought—"Heaven above you is only as wide as the earth beneath you."

We trudged our way closer to the sea's edge. We saw a majestic sight—a steamship sailing at ease, on troubled waters.

"There", my companion whispered, "is yet another sermon —in the language of men. Men search for peace among nations, between men, and in their minds, but they do not find it, for they seek the wrong kind of peace.

"They seek for a world or a soul without trouble or conflict. They multiply problems because they run away from problems. But all of life implies conflict.

"You cannot achieve peace by retreating from trouble—but only by resolving conflict."

Hope gathered in his patient eyes. "Look at that ship", he said. "Outwardly it is a picture of peace. Do you know why that is so? Because deep in her hold the engines are churning, motors are throbbing, resolving the conflict between ship and sea. Do not retreat to some never-never land where problems never grow. A world at ease is a world without peace."

When most people think of "peace of mind", they conjure up some never-never land where—
> there are no conflicts
> and children don't scream
> and the dogs don't bark or bite.

They dream of a world where—
> wives aren't cross
> and husbands don't shout
> and decisions can always be dropped in someone else's lap!

This is not peace of mind—it is the peace of the cemetery!

What is more: Peace emerges from the mature awareness that there are no perfect solutions, for all along the line people will err; and this being so, all along the line people must understand and forgive.

The trouble with many of us is that we have lost confidence in our ability to resolve conflict. But like Br'er Rabbit, man is "born and bred in a brier patch"! Throw him into the thorns and he will emerge, bruised and wounded. But he will emerge, nevertheless, because he is born into trouble "as the sparks fly upward".

Mental hospitals are filled with people who never recognized that fundamental reality of their own nature. Naturally, they were born into a world which is a world of conflict, and unnaturally they believe that only they were so condemned. They are not sick because of conflict; they are ill because they haven't learned how to live in spite of conflict.

The real world is one where decisions have to be made and unmade, where children are sick and do die, where the righteous suffer and the evil prosper. The living reality of human experience teaches us that ours is a world in which there are no final and comprehensive answers. There are only a series of ongoing and continuing questions.

The wise man is not the one who has all the answers; he is the man who recognizes the questions.

Ultimately, history teaches, every answer has produced a new question, because if it had not, it was really not a true answer. Every resolution of conflict must lead to a new approach, and every new approach must lead to a questioning of all that has come before. So long as we live, we live without finality. Only in the cemetery is there no conflict because the final answer has come.

Man is finite, but his problems infinite. He cannot solve all of his questions, because he can never possess all of the answers.

Real confidence comes to those who, lacking all of the answers, still learn how to live nobly by having learned how to live with their questions.

CONFIDENCE REQUIRES
OPTIMISTIC THINKING

To make his point, the teacher took a water tumbler and placed it in front of the class. He poured enough water into it to reach the middle of the glass. And then he began his experiment. Each student was asked to describe on a slip of paper what he saw.

When the papers were collected and read they revealed a truth the teacher was anxious to explain. About half the class described the glass as half-full. The others said the glass was half-empty.

Given the same set of facts, and the same opportunities, people will nevertheless differ. More than that: They will see life and its possibilities principally in terms of their own inner spirit. That is why even children of the same parents will often run entirely different gamuts of feeling and expression.

Some will tell us that we are what we eat. Perhaps. What is sometimes more significant is the fact that we are what we see. And it is the sight that comes from within us that makes us see. In a word, our "insight".

The difference between perennial optimists and pessimists, as with those students, is the result of what each group chooses to see of the world in which they live.

For some, life is but half-full, full of possibilities, full of unborn challenges to a more noble human adventure. For others, life is half-empty, devoid of meaning, a boring, humdrum round of vicious circles.

Consider Solomon. Tradition has it that he wrote three books. When he was young and full of the zeal of living, he hadn't yet seen life. He only heard of it. And for him, it was a sweet, uncomplicated melody. His first book, "Song of Songs", has echoed down the ages as a call to all the young in heart.

But years sharpened his experience and gave him the sophistication and sobriety that come with increased understanding.

He wrote his "Proverbs" in the middle years, in the fuller vigour of his insight. He still saw life's sweetness and fullness. But he also saw its sordidness. He came to look at different things.

While he still knew the meaning of love and pleasure and personal happiness, his eyes now caught the vision of the poor, the proud, the fools, and the fearful. He saw that there was more to life than himself.

But then he grew old. All of us grow older. But beware of growing old. Solomon's third book reminds us of the danger. In "Ecclesiastes" he sees only that all is vanity. Now there is nothing new under the sun. Life is empty.

If you want a good clue to his thinking, just count the frequency of his use of the pronoun "I". He's old because he just can't get himself off his mind.

These are the perils of seeing only ourselves:

When we're younger, we miss the real issues of living because we see life as full and final as long as we ourselves are happy.

When we grow old we often lose the joy of life. We see it empty and futile because we're sitting tightly on our hands.

True, no two people will see life the same. But the beginning of wisdom comes when we see life as only half-full and despite its problems never take our eyes off its possibilities. Confidence is built upon optimistic thinking.

B. PREPARE YOURSELF

BE YOURSELF OR BE LONELY

There were over 200 guests at the party. There was gaiety, laughter, stimulated joy, and wave after wave of small talk. The hostess moved politely from guest to guest, making the rounds.

The minister had come late, and so was virtually the last to leave. As he took his hat and was about to go, the hostess must have suddenly realized that the crowd had gone and that she was left all alone. And in a kind of half-musing, half-tragic way she said something like this:

"I feel sorry for them—all of them. For, I'm one of them. They spoke to me, and I spoke to every single one of them. But none of us heard. We all just spoke! I didn't enjoy myself and they didn't either. All of us were doing what we were expected to do. And now I'm all alone; but so were they. There were 200 people who crowded in here—but they were such a lonely crowd."

Most of the time we are bored and lonely because we simply go through our paces doing things we don't really believe in—doing them because we think that we must.

We're afraid of what people might say. We try to be what we are not because we are not sure of what we are. We are little people playing at the game of bigness, wearing masks which can't cover up the emptiness within. Only if we possess a personal sense of values can we be rescued from our sense of loneliness.

How do you measure a value? It isn't easy. Perhaps this incident in the life of Isaac Ben Zvi, president of the State of Israel, may tell us something about one man's value-scale.

Ben Zvi is essentially a scholar. After Dr. Weizmann died, he was elected president of Israel. Ben Zvi lived with his wife Rachel in a small hut in Jerusalem.

On the day that he was elected president, he returned home at night and found a sentry marching up and down in front of his hut. He asked what the purpose was. The young sergeant replied that he was sent by his chief of staff to do guard duty in front of the home of the president. Rubbing his head in amazement, Ben Zvi went into the house.

The night was cold; it was winter in Jerusalem. After a few minutes the president went out and said:

"Look here, it's cold tonight. Won't you come in and have some hot tea?"

The young soldier replied:

"I cannot leave my post. Orders are orders."

Foiled, the president re-entered his house. After a while, he turned to his wife and told her to make some tea. With that he went out again. Outside, turning to the soldier, he said earnestly:

"Look here, I've got an idea—you go in and have some tea and I'll stand outside with your gun and take your post!"

Here is a symbol of a man who is too big to be little, too humble to make himself falsely big. He wasn't afraid of what people might say. He cut through convention in order to do the right and human thing. Above all, he wasn't victimized by false, bedevilling pride. What made him president? The sentry patrolling in front of his hut, loudly clicking his heels?

Would the lack of one make him any less of a president?   Of course not!

We are lonely because we are too busy being what we are not. We never give ourselves the opportunity to get to know who and what we are or can be.

To many of us are faceless, nameless men lost in a lonely crowd of conformists. We become the easy victims of every passing fad, each maudlin fetish. We "hoola-hoop", "yo-yo" in required seasons; we shorten the "hem-lines" of our personality in accordance with the latest, official communiques. We don't "zig" when we are told to "zag"; we don't dare waltz in the age of the "cha-cha-cha". We even preach "togetherness" without practising it—in order to appear to be in style, saying what everyone seems to be saying.

We enjoy doing conventional things, even though we may complain about them, because in reality they save our lives. We cultivate so little personal originality that we cover ourselves up by what the crowd is doing. But nevertheless, lonely we remain, because we lack inner fulfillment.

Here is some basic advice: Cultivate your self-confidence by learning how to enjoy things which appeal to something that flows deeply within your own soul.   Be happy in the enjoyment of even the simple, quiet attainments—things that satisfy and that fulfill *you!*

LEARN NOT TO HATE

"He's not heavy, he's my brother!"

This legend beneath a poster showing a small boy carrying another lad who had been hurt is a good reminder of the meaning of brotherhood.

Human beings are remarkable. They alone of all creation have been endowed with the faculty of intellectual memory. And what a powerful instrument this is. Too often we remember only what we choose to remember and are forgetful of what we should remember.

If every group in this country would remember how, at some point in its history, it was maligned, misunderstood, and persecuted, it might learn how to live more happily with neighbours of different colours or creeds. There is no majority anywhere that sometime has not felt what it means to be in the minority.

The catacombs are eternal reminders to the Christian of his own minority status in the pre-Christian Roman world. For a Christian to persecute others because of their differences, or their small numbers, makes caricatures out of their own martyrs.

The blasted synagogues and the ashes of six million Jews who went to their doom in Hitler's Europe serve as a gaunt reminder for all Jews that the wages of hatred is death. No Jew can afford the immoral luxury of hating. Wars beget wars. So, hate begets hate.

The consequences of monotheism have not yet dawned upon the minds of most men—believers among them. To pray to One God is to affirm that all of His creatures are united under Him in one commonalty of humanity. That is why Christians or Jews who claim the universality of God blaspheme Him, not so much by words of heresy, as when they defame or revile the personality of their neighbours.

Man does not exist apart from fellow man. God cannot be a Father to men who are not brothers.

Jews have suffered much at the hands of the intolerant and the arrogant. Christians were crucified throughout the lands of the Roman Empire. All the more reason why more of us should not stoop to be conquered by the instruments of hate which have caused us hurt.

There's a text that sums all of this up very neatly, and it runs like a refrain through the Bible. It calls upon us to remember. Remember what? "Remember that you were slaves in the land of Egypt!" Every group has once been slaves. Every group longs for freedom. And there can only be freedom when there is liberty and justice for all.

This is why every one of us—Catholic, Protestant, and Jew— needs every one of us—Catholic, Protestant, and Jew.

When we learn not to hate, we grow in strength, in confidence, and in moral stature.

GIVE THE WORLD WHAT YOU HAVE TAKEN

"To plant a tree; to rear a child; to write a book."

One of the world's wise men called these three enterprises— these sacred, adventurous pursuits—the consummate goals of human aspirations. Each demands from us our deepest faith; a belief that what we are doing is supremely important. Each suggests that we become as concerned with what happens after we are gone as we are with our own lives.

In an ancient rabbinic legend, the story is told of a man who, already passed the normal span of three-score-ten, set out to plant little saplings. His friends remonstrated with him. They chided: "Why do you plant? Do you really believe that you will still be here to see the mighty trees which will arise?"

"Not at all," he replied, "yet I plant.

"I plant to offer their fruit and their shade, their beauty and their majesty to a generation yet unborn. For have I not enjoyed these very things from the hands of men whom I have never known or seen—men who planted for me?"

Every time we are moved to sow a seed for the long to-morrow, to plant the fruit for those who are yet to come, we become part of the eternal rhythm of the universe—we give back something of our own confidence and faith to a world from which we have received so much. Little enough repayment it is.

Yet, not everyone plants who sows. And this, for the same reason that not all who have children rear them. To plant a tree and to rear a child calls for a love which abides. Life grows only in response to concerns that continue; the tree which is not watered and the child that is not tenderly nurtured remain forever stunted. They are glaring reminders of what could have been; they literally stand as broken promises.

Their tragedy reflects our own: we had it within our power to help bring forth precious fruit, but our faith lacked stamina. It started brightly, but flickered and died. No need, then, to blame the unreared child any more than it is wise to castigate the stunted tree. Both are the product of inconstant love.

Of the making of books there is no end. But few are written which remain alive. A classic stays unforgettable because it has not deigned to deal with themes which are trivial. Love stories may be cheap—and when they are, they soon are tossed out of mind into the nearest receptacle.

Most "paper-backs" slickly roll off our spines—we are untouched and unmoved. But a great love story is a story of majesty and heroism, whose characters represent the grandeur of the human heart and the nobility of the human soul.

The story does not always end "happily ever after". But it remains with us ever after, when we have been brought face to face with people we can admire and respect.

Life, too, is a book we author. Long after we are gone, the "invisible writing" remains for others to read. If our concerns have been trivial, our themes irrelevant, our lives, too, will be quickly discarded, dumped upon the nearest scrap-heap. To write a book which will be read is not the challenge. Will it be remembered?

"To plant a tree; to rear a child; to write a book." Many do and many fail.

Will the tree you plant grow? It will, if you will grow, too. Will the child you produce be reared? He will, if you will rise to the height you have set for him.

Will your book be remembered? It will, if you, as the main hero, really become a hero.

MAKE LIFE A WINDOW, NOT A MIRROR

One day, a rich but unhappy man came to see his rabbi to discuss a question that deeply troubled him. He had everything and yet he had nothing. He wanted advice to help him get at the root of his difficulty.

The rabbi took him by the hand and led him to the window.

"Look out there", he said. And the rich man looked into the street.

"What do you see?" the rabbi asked.

"People", he answered, with a quizzical and confused look. Whereupon the rabbi took him by the hand again and this time led him to the mirror.

"What do you see now", he asked. "Now I see myself", the rich man answered. But still bewildered by the rabbi's approach to his problem, he cried out:

"But what does this have to do with my personal situation?"

"Just about everything", the rabbi replied. "In the window there is glass and in the mirror there is glass. But the glass in the mirror is covered with silver. And that's the heart of your difficulty. No sooner is silver added to the window glass, than you stop seeing others.

"All you can see is yourself. My friend, you had better start looking out the window and forgetting about the mirror, if you want to find a cure to your ills."

There is a pertinent lesson here for some of us. Our lives are without effect because we haven't a cause. Too many of us are comfortably wrapped up in our tight little islands, and as a result we're isolated from the mainland. We appear to be permanently snowed in and under.

Perhaps we are afraid that if we show some warmth, or interest in others, they may exploit us without end.

Maybe this is the reason too many of us permit our helpful instincts to become stunted; and we wilfully remain forever underdeveloped.

But it is difficult to find a person actively devoted to some idea or purpose which lifts him out of his own skin, who doesn't actually receive more than he ever could give.

For we are not meant to be lonely, or marooned. We come to our highest expression when we feel part of something useful and helpful. People need us, but we also need people.

Once, the tale goes, there was a leaf who pined for the

freedom of the birds that fluttered nearby. Every day he would watch them soaring on high, singing their songs as they flew.

If only he could cut himself loose from the branch that imprisoned him. If only a big wind would come and blow him into freedom, he too could soar and climb as he willed.

One day, his prayer was answered and a big wind came. Louder and louder it whined, until suddenly, with a mighty gust, it blew the leaf free from its mooring. For a fleeting moment the leaf was free. He was overcome with joy and gladness. But it wasn't long before he was flat on his back, an easy victim of the trampling of every passerby. Very soon his colour was gone, his strength was sapped, and his hope lost. He died seeking the wrong kind of happiness.

The poor leaf didn't know what some of us don't know. To achieve inner strength we have to be attached to some life-giving force. The moment we cut ourselves off from great causes and concerns, and begin thinking of ourselves alone, we fall prey to our own pettiness and become weak.

Like coupons, we are just "not good if detached."

KNOW THE LIMITS OF FREEDOM

He whose self-glory fills his gaze never sees the sun shine.

And there's much to pity. For, too many "free men" don't know the meaning of their freedom. That's the reason why instead of being truly free, the lives of some men are filled with a confusion born of anarchy.

The freest man is the one who understands that he is not a law unto himself. He recognizes and yields to the higher laws of life that go far beyond himself.

We don't willingly defy the laws of gravity. When we do, we do it at the peril of our life. So, too, the wise man knows the limits of his own freedom and he learns to co-operate with God's laws in nature.

If you and I were to depend upon our individual ideas in digging a tunnel, we might well quarrel over which of us was right and be quickly smothered by a cave-in. But if both of us follow the methods of a civil engineer, no such argument could develop.

Starting from opposite sides of the Hudson River, the Holland Tunnel met to the fraction of one inch. Here was a magnificent example of obedience to the laws of nature.

The venture was successful because behind it was the surrender of the freedom of personal whim to the dictates of a higher law which governed the engineers.

Ultimately, there is no freedom save in obedience to the eternal rhythms of life. There is no peace until one yields to a law that transcends the self. Good judgment is the result of our ability to weigh our own desires against our responsibilities, our own drives against the demands upon us of the higher laws of life.

To achieve this in our personal life we must become intelligently mature. He who is willing to surrender his pride before the dictates of judgment has become a man.

Personal pride is against nature, for it inclines the individual to demand his own way. And when everybody wants to have it his way alone, no one is truly free.

Thus, the spectre of the "self-made" man is frightening to behold; he is a human caricature. He thinks he's free but he's self-enslaved.

Instead, we should strive to become a "co-operative man". We prepare ourselves for confident living when we lose our selves serving God and our fellow man.

DEVELOP THE COURAGE OF KINDNESS

When they opened the diary of a renowned ethical teacher, they searched for a clue to his thoughts. But all pages of the book were blank, save one. And on this page there was inscribed a note in a few short lines. This is the sum of it:

"Before you speak or act, ask yourself three questions: Is it true? Is it necessary? Is it kind? And the last is not the least but the most."

There is no substitute for the truth. It has a way of catching up with us. No matter how difficult to face, truth always gives us healing power. When we deal honestly with people, we feel "clean inside". Armed with a potent weapon, we have the confidence to face our problems.

But truth alone will not do. When we ask ourselves what we are doing, we must consider: Is it kind as well as true?

William Blake, the English poet, reminds us that "a truth that's told with bad intent, beats all the lies you can invent."

Some people, like Uriah Heep, deal with their neighbours in a smug, self-righteous way. They act as if no one else is honest and only they have cornered the market on truth. We've got to deal truthfully with people, but kindly as well.

And when we set about saying or doing the things we deem necessary, let's also remember to be kind.

Consider what we do as parents. Of course we must assert our leadership and help our children make wise choices. A parent who lets his children flounder about without guiding them has missed the whole point of parenthood.

But too many parents forget that their children are human

beings. Too often they make all of the decisions for their children, instead of making decisions with them.

Instead of leadership, there is dictation, and in the place of kindly light, there is wooden command. The parent may think that he's only doing what is necessary! Yes, that's all he's doing—and forgetting to be kind.

Or think of some husbands you know. A man may suppose that he is doing everything that is necessary to please his wife. He earns a decent salary; he provides a nice house; he even offers his wife a long vacation. He thinks that he's doing "everything that is necessary and then some".

But if in the process he forgets to be kind, sweet, and understanding, then he's forgotten what is really most necessary. And since marriage is a two-way street, what's true of the gander is true of the goose.

Or ponder the primary and ultimate cause for failure of communism, fascism, or any of the assorted totalitarian forms of government. The leaders may be stoutly convinced of the truth and necessity of their plans and programs, but they have not sufficient confidence in the effectiveness of these two weapons of truth and necessity to work with them in kindly fashion.

They have forgotten the meaning of kindness and elementary humanity. And when they've lost this, they've lost everything.

No matter where you apply it—in the family, community, or nation—that teacher summed it up neatly:

"Is it true? Is it necessary? Is it kind? And the last is not the least but the most."

FACE SORROWS HEROICALLY

After the atomic explosion had blasted Hiroshima, one man who survived without injury went visiting the maimed and the dying, and to each he apologized for not being hurt, too.

To everyone who has ever been bereaved, who has suffered the loss of a beloved, the vision of this man suggests a profoundly moving and helpful thought.

Our ancestors seemed to know better than we that death is part of life's span. That's because they had a faith that helped them face death as well as life. They came to understand that while faith of itself did not give them all of the answers, it offered something fundamental and necessary. It taught them how to view life's problems.

While we moderns are still very certain of the inevitability of taxes, we often act as if we no longer held such a view regarding death.

Grief is a spiritual malady and we learn one of its cures when we recognize that death and sorrow are universal. What is it that makes us respond with sympathy to that man of Hiroshima? From him we can begin to understand that there are times in life when it is possible to feel guilty because we have been spared the universal fate of other men.

And out of this understanding, when we ponder life carefully, there often comes the recognition that even if all is well with us we must suffer because of the suffering of others.

And if we know sorrow because others know it, we also will know how to respond to it when it strikes at our own door.

Consider what happened to another man. He was in an automobile accident and in his convalescence was required to walk on crutches. For the first time in his life, he said, he noticed how many cripples there were.

And so it can be with all of us. When death or tragedy comes, and fate compels us to use crutches, there are two courses we can take:

We can go all to pieces, pitying ourselves and seeking the sympathy of our neighbours. Or, we can forget our own crutches and see how many other people are limping.

If we follow the second course, we will find still another cure to that spiritual malady known as grief. We'll learn to give up concentrating on our feeling and go on to some kind of active doing. We get some help even if we do no more than attend to the ordinary affairs of living.

But more than this, if we are identified with some great cause, we are bound to receive in return infinitely more than we possibly can give—in satisfactions, fulfillments, and the joys that come from serving an ideal.

Sorrow's effect, it has been said, is like that of intense cold.

When Napoleon's soldiers were retreating from Moscow, they paused to rest by the side of the road. They sought to take but a moment's sleep. But some never awoke. They were frozen stiff.

If we do not know how to treat it, sorrow can be like the bitter cold of a northern winter. Stay inactive, keep telling yourself how terrible you feel, never get up and do, and you are lost—to yourself and to everyone else.

You've got to march on! You'll learn how by keeping your eye and your heart on the suffering in the world around you.

When we face sorrow heroically, marching on to keep pace with life's demands, we gain confidence by comforting others.

C. WORK WITH OTHERS

CULTIVATE PITY AND COMPASSION

The man was shaking with rage. He was thoroughly angry. He was going to get his revenge, he said.

"Nobody's going to do that sort of thing to me and get away with it!"

When, at last, some quiet words could be spoken, a friend suggested:

"If you really want to take revenge on him and not on yourself, why not try a little pity. You'd be amazed how much good it will do the both of you!"

Nature teaches a lesson about human nature. A certain species of bee is equipped with a powerful stinger. But it is so constructed physically that once the bee stings, it dies.

And so with us. When we persist in hurting others, we destroy something good within ourselves.

Many of us have been hurt by malicious slander, caustic gossip, and a variety of betrayed loyalties. When we think of these things, we become bitter with resentment. But the real answer is not more hate, more hurt, more gossip and slander. The answer is pity.

This is a religious teaching. But it is buttressed by psychological finds, as well. The psychologists don't call it pity or sympathy; they call it empathy.

They suggest that we get inside the feelings of the offending person, see how he feels, and get to know his shortcomings.

When we do this, he can't possibly hurt us, for we've come to see how miserable he is himself. Instead of hating him, we will pity him. And pity will teach us to bury the hatchet by trading anger for compassion.

This is the way the strong remain strong—by using no weapons save an understanding of weakness. For to understand is to forgive.

If others have wronged us, before striking back, we ought to remember that we have also hurt people.

And let's not add still another victim to our list. When you fight fire with fire, you've got to increase the area of destruction.

Forgive, if you cannot forget! This is a lesson which maturity teaches. It is sometimes a costly lesson, a lesson for which many of us pay dearly—sometimes at the price of our happiness.

We are prevented by our pride from doing that which reason would have us do. Our false dignity mocks us, and makes dwarfs of people who could behave much bigger.

Here are a man and wife, tormented by a hate which is the product of trivia. Harsh words, caustic looks, hurtful remarks: These are the ingredients of a house of woe, unnecessarily destroying itself.

Add or multiply examples; they abound heavily on all sides. We could be a lot happier if we uncluttered our hearts and minds and cleaned away some of the cobwebs of suspicion, distrust, and skepticism.

Man's mind is a double-edged sword. It remembers the bad and it prods him not to forget the good. But too frequently, we "remember too much"—we linger overlong on the hurt that some have caused us, without seeking the healing we need.

There comes a time in our lives when we seek forgiveness for the things we have done or left undone. And when this happens, a light sometimes dawns. We discover an ancient truth: He who seeks forgiveness finds it only by being forgiving of others.

LIVE CHARITABLY

Words are important not only for what they mean but for what they don't mean.

Take the word *charity*. The dictionary will tell you that charity is synonymous with almsgiving. But when the Hebrew Bible used that word it meant something entirely different.

Charity was first and foremost an attitude towards life, based upon righteousness and justice. What a world of difference between that and the dictionary definition.

If charity is but the offering of alms to the needy, it is an affair of the heart, a sweet sentiment of pity. But only a sentiment.

The fluttering heart may utter its heavy sighs. And for a fleeting flash we are seized by an overwhelming mood of mercy. So we drop our coins or write our cheques and we are done. We return quickly to our business as usual.

Some of us are overcome by our own mercy. We even talk about our "charity", and sometimes seek recognition for it. After all, we learn to tell ourselves, we really didn't have to do it!

But when the Bible speaks of charity, it has something else in mind. Charity isn't optional any more than is justice.

You don't give charity, you live charitably.

You're not charitable because you're a big-hearted fellow who does more than he should. You're charitable only when you do what you know you must do.   Charity isn't a gift, it's a deed.

"I was taught", one man complained, "that if I learned to do the right thing, I would gain the secret of happiness and achieve the serenity which goodness brings.   I have not found this to be true.   I am tired of doing the right things when I don't get rewards I believe I'm entitled to!"

"I see your difficulty," his friend replied.   "There is something much deeper that you have not learned.   It is not enough to *do* the right things.   If you seek happiness and personal fulfillment, you must learn to *enjoy* doing them!"

Here is the real significance of charity: The joyful giver is grateful for not having to receive.   He delights in taking tokens of his own blessing and putting out his hand in helpfulness. But even giving, it has been wisely said, is not the real essence of charity; it is the delicacy of our feeling that counts.   For the Scripture does not say, "Happy is he who giveth to the poor", but rather, "Happy is he who wisely considereth the poor."

Regrettably, modern philanthropy often misses the spiritual mark.   Many people do acts of charity.   But how many enjoy doing them?   So many of us strike bargains with conscience, and "give charity", as if it were a kind of trade or transaction arranged with an eye to the balance sheet.   Righteous acts of charity, done mechanically, unaccompanied by the thrill of helpfulness and the sense of humanity which come from participating in another's need, can only lead to boring and dull self-righteousness.

"I did my duty, didn't I?"   One can hear on all sides this famous complaint of "unhappy saints".   The point is: How did you do your duty? Listlessly and methodically? Only because you could not retreat from it?   Or was there something singing within you?   Was there an inner buoyancy, a spiritual delight which continues to glow even in the darkest hours?

Seven hundred and fifty years ago, a teacher and physician named Maimonides died. In his lifetime he wrote books on religion, medicine, and philosophy. One of the most significant things he wrote related to charity. Here are his words:

"There are eight degrees in charity, one higher than the other:

"He who gives grudgingly, reluctantly, or with regret.

"He who gives grudgingly, but gives graciously.

"He who gives what he should, but only after he is asked.

"He who gives before he is asked.

"He who gives without knowing to whom he gives, although the recipient knows the identity of the donor.

"He who gives without making his identity known.

"He who gives without knowing to whom he gives, neither does the recipient know from whom he receives.

"He who helps a fellow man to support himself."

Note the highest degree. It is an act that abolishes the need for the dictionary's "charity" because it is conceived in the spirit of Biblical charity. Charity is an act of justice; it is an act of faith and confidence in the moral law.

Charity begins at home? Indeed. But only when it is this kind of charity.

RECOGNIZE THE MEANING OF EQUALITY

The rabbis of old tell a quaint story. They try to explain why it was that Cain slew Abel. The text itself gives no immediate clue. Cain and Abel had the whole world before them and yet the first child became the first murderer.

And in a fanciful moral teaching, the rabbis explain that Cain and Abel agreed that each would take half the world.

Soon Cain proposed to Abel that they build a temple to God. Then Cain announced to Abel that he would build a temple to God in his part of the world and Abel proposed to do the same.

Nothing would have been wrong if each had built, in his own way, a temple to God. Apparently, they did not see it this way. Each claimed God for himself. So Cain rose up and slew Abel. All this, in the name of God. The story is still being re-enacted in our time.

Perhaps for this reason another story is recounted soon thereafter: The story of the Tower of Babel. The Bible is very explicit in explaining the purpose of this moral lesson: "And the whole earth was of one language and of one speech."

When this happened, men began to feel that they had a monopoly on truth, and so they thought to build a tower with its top in Heaven. Again the vision of man's essential equality was ignored. For only they were to build a tower; they would not permit the generations which would come after them to build it. So God scattered them over the face of the earth— with different languages and creeds.

The story of the Tower of Babel indicates the great paradox of human existence: While we are all made of the same stuff, there is room for difference. Nay, there is blessing in differences. We are one but many. We are the same, but each is unique.

Here is the real meaning of the democratic dream. And it goes back to still another Biblical teaching. Micah said it:

"Nation shall not lift up sword against nation. Neither shall they learn war any more. But they shall sit every man under his vine and his fig tree. And none shall make them afraid. For let all people walk each one in the name of its God."

Who are the fearful? Those who want all to conform to their own viewpoint. Who are the weak? Those who believe

in the power of material strength alone.   Who are the ungodly?
Those who let no one else walk in the name of their own God.

This is the democratic vision and the real meaning of
spiritual brotherhood.   It is derived from the dream and the
hope of the good for the many.   Does this not mean that we
shall survive only when we are committed to a moral way of
life?   Does this not mean that the only way we can win the
heart of the world to this democratic dream is by acting in a
moral manner?

We must alter our thinking if we are to win the world to our
dream and our vision.   We shall not win by relying on our
might and our force.   Only when we recognize that we must
stake our hopes on the moral decision of human equality can
we be true to our vision.

The vision is a radical idea.   True democracy embodies one
of the greatest revolutionary forces in human history, going
back on a straight line to Micah: "For let all people walk
each one in the name of its God."

Today, throughout the communities of North America we
are witnessing a kind of religious revival.   But it will not long
endure if it is based upon denominational factors alone.   Only
when churches and synagogues use their vision to speak to men,
not only for the sake of preserving their own tradition, but also
to help realize that over-arching community which is one, can
religion truly be godly.

When men do not fear each other, when man may sit under
his vine and his fig tree, and nations do not learn war any more,
then will they never destroy each other.

We need to learn to respect the conscience of men as much
as we fear their differences.   Man's strength does not come
from subduing his neighbour; it derives from his ability to
conquer his own base passions and recognize the equality of all
men.

LEAD THROUGH HUMILITY

Followers blame leaders. They often seek more than they can ever receive. They look to them for inspiration, for facile answers, for big solutions, and they are often left wanting. The truth of the matter is that every generation gets the kind of leadership it deserves. What is more: leadership is a function of discipleship. When the mass is uninspired, leadership will be uninspiring. When the average man seeks no solutions from within himself, he can rarely find it in others.

One sage put his finger on the nub of the matter. "Why", he queried, "am I not as great a master as Moses? If I had had the teacher he had, I, too, could have been a Moses!" And then he proceeded to answer his own question: "But why did I not have a teacher like Moses? Probably because I am not as good a student as Moses!"

Teachers are elevated by their students, as followers shape and mold their leaders. And all require at least three essential personal qualities: humility, totality, and continuity.

Some people are purely vocal in their leadership, instead of being instrumental. The true leader recognizes that he is not an end in himself; he is a channel, an instrument, a vessel leading towards a goal. Wherever you find greatness, there you also find humility; they are twins. The great man can afford to be humble because he knows that he himself and those who follow are equal servants to a cause. Unfortunately, too many followers of would-be great men initiate the latter's decline and degeneration by vulgarizing concepts of leadership; they cause leaders to believe themselves to be demi-gods worshipping at their own shrine, instead of serving the greater goal.

There is also too much partial leadership: those who are only partly committed to an idea cannot serve it totally. They see it only from a fragmentary angle of vision; they lack the whole view, the broad outlook, the big picture.

Continuity, as well, is a must for the effective pursuit of an ideal. Presidents of organizations, chairmen of committees who drop their commitments at the end of their term of office may be good technicians; they surely are not great leaders. Leadership is not merely an ecstasy or a glorious insight; it should include these, but it requires much more.

Real leadership asks us to maintain a confident loyalty to the causes we serve. Flashes in the pan may be brilliant; they are, however, too quickly and easily consumed. We do not possess leadership unless we are permanently possessed by our visions.

If disciples want these qualities in their masters and teachers, they had better begin acquiring some for themselves!

BECOME A REAL BROTHER

Do's and don'ts!

We can be helped by them in the task of learning how to get along with people of different faiths, cultures, and national backgrounds. Here is a list of six which may help to turn heat into light, enemies into friends, skepticism into confidence:

1. Don't generalize from isolated particulars.

Too many people draw irresponsible conclusions from individual experiences. Having had a bad run-in with a human being of another faith, they conclude erroneously that all people of that faith are as bad as the one, or two, that they have met.

Human beings, even those of the same faith or cultural background, differ broadly, each from the other. They must be judged on no other basis than what they are themselves. Many people falsely believe that members of groups other than their own "are all alike".

The late Dr. Stephen Wise once jocularly replied to such nonsense by suggesting, as regards his own group, that "the only thing that two people can easily agree upon is what the third should give to charity."

What is true of Jews, in this respect, is equally true of Catholics, Protestants, Moslems, or agnostics.

2. Don't underestimate your neighbour.

As proponents of democracy we surely do not agree with the political and social doctrines of the Russian people. But this should not suggest the absurdity that only the Western peoples have advanced scientifically and technologically—and not the people behind the Iron Curtain.

Many of us have succumbed to the false notion that when we deride the next fellow, we automatically inflate ourselves. We have recently discovered, to our misfortune, that the West does not gain when it simply berates the East.

The West can only advance when it is prepared to accept what others can do because it has confidence in what it itself can do. This truth applies with equal force to the people who make up our own communities. Don't talk them down believing that you are talking yourself up.

3. Don't ask more for yourself than you are willing to extend to others.

We have the unhappy faculty of demanding equality when we seek it; yet we act as though we were "more equal" than others.

The well-known quotation of the Book of Leviticus has been translated from the Hebrew as "Love thy neighbour as thyself." The original text really reads: "Love thy neighbour; he is as you are."

If he is as you are, then surely you are as he is. If you want liberty, affection, and respect for yourself, you must be prepared to offer it in equal measure to those around you, who usually want it as much as you do.

And now, for three Commandments of a positive nature:

A. Do familiarize yourself with the life and the hopes of the people who are different from you.

It has been said that familiarity breeds contempt. Perhaps the opposite is closer to the truth: Familiarity breeds understanding. When we get to know more about the kind of life led by those not of our own faith and not of our own culture, we become citizens of the world, recognizing the profound quality which every group possesses—not only our own.

B. Do criticize yourself before you judge others.

We are more prone, when we are thoughtless, to do otherwise. Too often we indulge ourselves while judging others. We ought to try to cultivate the sounder habit: To judge ourselves while seeking to understand others. Such a habit, if adopted by all, might lead to a saner relationship with ourselves as well as with others.

C. Do respect the merit of the individual regardless of the group which he represents.

When you must judge, judge the individual not the group. Society requires us to live together in groups and to foster our personalities by important contacts with groups—yet no man is a group; he is himself.

High religion teaches that each of us is made in the image of God. This is a necessary reminder that each man is a world unto himself: unique, complex, and puzzling; but potentially good, and perhaps even great. Destroy a man and you destroy a whole world!

A little girl was given a jigsaw puzzle by her father. He wanted her to learn the map of the world in this easy, educational manner. Unknown to him, on the underside of the puzzle there was a picture of a man. When the child came to report her success to her father, he wondered how it was that she had put the puzzle together in such short order. She explained: "You see, Daddy, all I had to do was to put the man together and the whole world came together!"

What that youngster said needs to be repeated by each of us. The world cannot be brought together until each man attempts to put himself together. Understanding, love, and brotherhood never begin somewhere else unless they first begin with ourselves.

DISCOVER LOVE

"What endures?" asked the rabbis of old.
And in this quaint way they answered their question:
Rock is strong but iron cleaves it.
Fire melts iron.
Water extinguishes fire.
Clouds come and bear water aloft.
But the wind drives clouds away.
Man may withstand wind.
But fear unmans man.
Wine can dispel fear.
But sleep overcomes wine.
And death sweeps away even sleep.
"What then endures?"
"Only love. For love and deeds of loving kindness defy and survive death."

Man dies for want of love. We may be chastised and cruelly hurt but as long as someone loves us we can keep on going as if everyone did. And as with all spiritual gifts, the more we give of love, the more we get. The more we share, the more there is to keep.

Some people are admired but not loved, others are respected yet not trusted, and still others are obeyed with trembling. But little remains of them after they're gone. They pan out in a flash. Their memories go up in smoke.

But those who are beloved endure as a blessed influence in the lives they have touched. For to be loved one must be loving. And he is loving who has touched and moved the hearts of others.

Too few of us know that kind of love. Often, we are miserly with our deepest affection. We have it, as it were, for the rainy day that never comes.

Sometimes it is too late. We vainly wish we could turn back the clock and tell those we really loved how much we loved them. But they are gone, and we stand empty-handed. We've cheated ourselves of one of the thrilling adventures of life.

Some of us never experience the joy of loving because we're over-concerned with the exchange rate. Before we give too much of ourselves we want to know "what's in it for me?"

But the life of love endures because it has conferred love freely. Its mercies and kindnesses are enshrined in deeds which have become living memorials. They were done for goodness's sake.

Mature love is principally a positive attitude towards life. Infantile, immature lovers think of love in terms of personal happiness, in the form of specific objects. They love "this man", "this woman", "this home", "this farm", "this community", "this land".

Profound espousal of life, which is the highest form of love, is not an affection that we have for specific things, alone. It can proclaim, even in the face of personal hurt: I want to help things grow; I want to see the seed take root; I want to help life aspire.

This is the kind of love which is at the heart of real faith. It unshackles the chains of our own personality and leads us to a world larger than our own ego.

This is why we remember our parents long after they have gone. For they loved us for what we were; just because we were. Not for what they could get out of us. One suspects that all they wanted was our love in return. And perhaps this is what all of us need more than we know: To love others because of interior, not ulterior, motives.

This kind of love comes into our lives the moment we understand how much we, too, depend upon it for survival. The commandment doesn't read "Love thy neighbour", but, "Love thy neighbour as thyself."

If you want to be loved—and who does not—you had better start loving people as you want to be loved yourself.

Part V

GUIDE YOUR FAMILY
TO A
CONFIDENT LIFE

FAMILIES NEED LOVE

Nothing we do in life, no matter how vaunted, adventure-some, or socially courageous, can replace the need each of us has for someone who loves us and who cares. Ideals are indeed important and, in some respects, indispensable, for a full life. But if we lack what we need so deeply as human beings—a sense of being uniquely important because we are uniquely loved—ideals in themselves can not satisfy our profound needs. It is all well and good to tell people who lack love or who have not known it, to lose themselves in their devotion to work or in their dedication to community welfare. Unfortunately, we are not so constructed. We still require people—not just ideas; human beings—not concepts alone, to satisfy our needs.

Despite all of the love we lavish upon the world, there is no substitute for the love we must share in our own homes. Jimmy Porter, in the play *Look Back In Anger*, condemns his wife for not sending flowers to the graveside of his friend's mother, because Jimmy Porter loved his friend's mother very deeply. But what he forgot was that no love for a friend's mother can really mean very much, if there is no deep love for your own wife. He was cruel to his wife in his own way, although surely he thought he loved her. But how could his wife love someone whom he wanted her to love when, in the first instance, he did not love her as she wanted him to love her? Our own homes are the laboratories of our lives. What we do there determines basically what we do when we leave home. That is why, despite all new inventions and modern designs, fads and fetishes, no one has yet invented, or will ever invent, a satisfying substitute for one's own family.

If you are fortunate enough to have a family, to have your loved ones with you and near you, do not let the opportunity slip through your fingers before it is too late. Unfortunately, some people have so taken their families for granted that they no longer enjoy best possible relations with their own relations. Brothers argue and refuse to speak. Sisters quarrel and go into temper tantrums. Parents and children divide off because of some stupid financial question. And all of us go off seeking new heroes, new examples, new models, and new friendships.

The eternal anecdotes and jokes concerning in-laws are too often more serious than comical. One wonders how we can expect to achieve respect in the eyes of our own children when we do not accord it to those who are our parents by marriage. You are a parent—so are the parents of your husband, of your wife! Some day they will be gone, gone forever, and then all kinds of guilt feelings will assert themselves—feelings that you did not do what you could have done at the time these things were possible. Some day when your beloved are gone forever, your own children will bear towards you the attitudes which you showed their grandparents.

All the friends we have acquired, the neighbours we have known, the associates with whom we identify ourselves, can never replace the need for family love. We need a home because we need a place where we can be just what we are, a place for natural and simple affections: no show, no veneered attempt at impressing others! We need a spot on earth where the door is always open to us, where people can laugh with us, but also wipe away our tears when we must cry. We need the warmth of people who have watched us grow up, who have suffered with us, and who have shared with us as no one has.

And if we were wise, we would act now on our noblest impulses. Today is all we have. Someday, we, too, will be part of yesterday. Share your love now, while there is time.

HUSBANDS NEED WIVES

A bargain has occasionally been reported—a bargain struck between a husband and wife, after long years of taunting.

In response to his wife's protestations over the arduousness of housework and its assorted menial chores, a husband trades his job with his wife: He will stay home for one week, taking care of the children, the kitchen, the lawn, the marketing, dusting, and cleaning, while she is to trot daily to the office, to run the factory, hire the help, cajole the customers, and outsmart the competitors.

Inevitably, at week's end, both are grateful for their rightful places, undoubtedly prepared to praise their Maker with psalms of thanksgiving for having made them what they are.

Knowing what we are, recognizing our frailties and our strengths, understanding our functions and our role in life is profoundly important.

Consider our role as parents: The most radical revolt of the twentieth century has been "the home revolution". And this, primarily because of the emancipation of the modern woman. But, frankly, to what purpose some of the fussing and the fuming of the unshackled female? If woman has been freed to do a man's job, who benefits?

We can agree that correction of the past was much required. Women are not chattel, pieces of property, nor pawns of power. A new perspective was needed, a balance required to assert for woman a more significant place in human affairs.

Ironically, however, in modern woman's quest for emancipation, the pendulum has swung to an absurd extreme. Becoming equal to man has made her want to be just like man.

Take our homes as prime examples. Man may build a house but it is woman who builds the home. She can transform brick and mortar into a sturdier and more lasting monument—character.

If women truly understood their special magic, their happy uniqueness, they would begin re-dedicating their quest for freedom in a broader dimension: They would seek the freedom to be themselves.

Women are needed more than ever in our society to be the taste-makers, the soft refiners of our homes. Man will ever be concerned with bread; woman must help him to remember that he does not live by bread alone. Man will always be concerned with livelihood; woman must, more than ever, remind him about the meaning of life. Man will seek to run faster and faster; woman must become the brake, to teach him that the race is not to the swift.

In a society which calls gold that which glitters, we make much of the dross, ignoring the essence. We respond to the sensational with mad affection, overlooking the quiet, unassuming virtues of life.

Indeed, this is what makes for the rapid "ups and downs" of our desires. Today, we "adore", "idolize", and "worship" the latest gods—of fashion, of literature, of stage and screen.

We carelessly invest our emotions in these dying deities, only to awake on the morrow to discover that they are already dead and buried. And so the bedeviled rush for new affections begins anew.

Despite our protests that we have no time, we are ready to begin the mad run all over again! And so it goes—on and on and on.

For these, and still other reasons, our communities are replete with mothers who find no adventure in raising children, and continually search for the "exciting", the "dramatic" roads to escape; living fathers who have orphaned their children by becoming machines, bigger cogs in the industrial wheels, in their mad dash from home; and thousands upon thousands of Joneses, keeping up with other Joneses, who have long ago forgotten with whom they are supposed to be keeping up.

One day, we will awake and discover that for all of our haste, we have not been moving ahead. We have been stuck in reverse gear, retreating all the time.

When we awake to that reality, we will begin to understand that our speed is not quite as important as our direction.

In a very real way woman is the last hope for man. When she becomes just like a man, she is no better than him. She must become better if he is to become better.

CHILDREN NEED GROWING PARENTS

Speak to parents and you will soon get the impression that something has gone wrong with modern children. "What can you do with them?"—this seems to be the universal, almost agonizing cry of embattled fathers and mothers. But if something has gone wrong with our children is there not the faintest possibility that something has, in the first instance, gone wrong with ourselves? Are we parents really communicating? Perhaps we are really not saying very much!

Is not much of our difficulty as parents born of the fact that children are really hero-worshippers, who must stop worshipping the hero when he no longer serves as the model for their lives? Are not many of the problems which exist between parents and growing children in our society the result of parents who have lost contact with the poetical and the psychological needs of our children? We clothe them, we house them, we feed them!

But do we inspire them? Is there much about us that they would like to emulate?

It is not unusual for a little girl of four or five to say that when she grows up she is going to marry her daddy, or for a boy to think similarly regarding his mother. As our children grow older and are drawn away from the binding circle of intimate family life, when they begin to take new flights with new-grown wings beyond the home, into the wider world—do they still find in us, their parents, the pattern of life worthy of emulation? Not too often.

And why not? Principally, because most of us shut the world out of our view and are self-imprisoned. While our children are growing and aspiring, we are declining, grinding away at our same, little preoccupations. Our children are being taught to read, to think more clearly, to meet the bigger world outside; and we have reached our peak and struggle to maintain our status quo.

Sometimes, as parents, we wonder why our children rebel against our authority and yet seem quite prepared to follow the dictates of others—of friends, teachers, neighbours. Said one father recently, "Why does my child listen to his scout leader, and will not listen to me?" "Well," came the reply, "what have you done with him lately?" We do not lead our children merely by asserting authority. We lead our children best when we participate in the life of our children.

CHILDREN NEED HEROES

Adolescents "are human beings", it has been said, "in the most awkward, unreasonable, and cantankerous stage."

No one seems to know what they might do next and no one is really capable of predicting what will happen to them, when they actually do it.

Why are adolescents such a problem? What is all the talking about? Why are they a problem no matter how intelligent or hardworking their parents may be? The answer to this question borders on the realm of religious insight, into the nature of man, into his deficiencies as well as his opportunities.

One needs to have a clear understanding of the needs of human beings as they grow through the various stages of life. As human beings develop, they disclose four successive needs.

First, of course, they need a vast amount of physical care. As soon as a baby is born, this need is most obvious and quite apparent. It is quite fortunate for the future of civilization that babies are attractive and usually "melt our hearts", for as a result parents will do anything in return for even a simple, toothless grin.

But there is a second need which manifests itself as children continue to grow. This is the need for confidence. Our children need a home in which they may feel safe. As much as our physical nourishment, they need our spiritual protection.

We, too, are clearly dependent upon others to help us, guide us, and minister to us. Our very lives depend upon those who are dependable. Always, of course, there is a need for love —not only for protection, discipline, or the rigour of parental authority—but for vast and continuing amounts of love.

This is an acute need which all of us have, except that children need more of it. Every person must have someone who deeply cares, who has a profound and abiding concern for him. Without love, life dries up on the vine; queer personality traits develop. This is clearly discernible in a child who has lost his parents or whose parents are cold and indifferent.

There is still another need which makes its appearance after the teenage years commence. Just as it is necessary for children to have care, protection, and love, to have parents who are utterly reliable and upon whom the child can really depend, so, when the age of puberty sets in, we find the need asserting itself, in the child, for an increasing amount of independence. Why does this take place? Because nature is trying to prepare the child for the next stage in his career.

Life consists of three significant and basic ages: the "age of dependence", which is our childhood; the "age of independence", which is our adolescence; the "age of inter-dependence", which is our maturity and the time for marriage. Yet, it should be obvious to all of us, that one can never become a free and inter-dependent person without first learning the meaning of independence.

The adolescent's increasingly vigorous demands for independence, his insistence on establishing his own identification as a person, are bound to create conflict with his parents, who, after all, are the symbols of authority to him. It is against authority that he is revolting, and the nearest ones at hand are his own parents.

As we move from childhood into puberty, we experience a new and glowing power. We are given bigger wings and we begin to take solo flights, testing our strength.

Adolescence is a time of life when we learn to cut the umbilical cord of dependence. Our independence takes a variety of forms. We kick and sputter. We clamour for attention. We are, at times, over-confident and, at other times, deeply afraid. We are self-conscious, because we are just becoming a self.

Physically, adolescence is a strange and wonderful time of our lives. We learn the meaning of being a somebody instead of a something. And spiritually, too, it is a great period. It is a time of protest, of idealism, of burning zeal—a time when we seek to find the "unadulterated truth". Through our storm and stress we are looking for the rainbow at the edges of the horizon.

But life has more to offer us than a chance at self-rule and sovereign independence. As we grow still older, some of us recognize the final need and goal of human experience. Marriage helps supply the clue to the secret.

There has never been a really successful marriage which wasn't based on mutual understanding and confidence, upon a shared recognition of inter-dependence. .

This is the lesson about life we are offered as we reach maturity. Man was not created to remain forever infantile, forever dependent upon others—lacking self-confidence— forever an object and never a subject.

But neither was he made to stay permanently juvenile, divorced from others, vain in his over-confidence, and ruggedly independent, measuring life only as it suits his own whims.

As parents we must seek to establish a hero pattern worthy of our children's emulation. This is the way we develop our children's confidence in us, even though, as independent persons, they must grow away from us.

Children cannot be easily fooled. They have microscopic eyes. Tell them to behave in a certain pattern which you have staked out for them, and then violate even one of your own rules, and they will detect who you are and what you are. Every child finds his parents out, some day.

When what you say may be measured by what you do, when you evoke a loving response in their lives by the way in which you live your own, you can long remain the loving hero of your children's dreams.

CHILDREN NEED SINCERITY

Two words tell the story of one of the most important questions we ever shall be called upon to answer.

The question is: How do we shape the lives of our children? And the words are "Personality" and "Sincerity".

"Personality" stems from a Latin word which means the "mask that actors wear". A good number of our "personality" problems are tied closely to this question. Instead of possessing character, we wear a "personality". We are not really what we seem to be. We carry masks that are easily donned and doffed.

But if we are to be real parents, guiding our children to confident living, we have to learn the vital ways of influencing them. And we influence not so much by what we say as by what we do. Ironically, you can't kid kids!

Equally important is the matter of feelings. We cannot feel one way and act another and leave our children in anything but open confusion.

There is more imparting of sentiment and molding of lives in one honest example than in 1,000 words of preachment.

In ancient Rome, outside the studios of some sculptors, there hung the sign "Sine cera"—without wax. Why? Because if a sculptor chipped away too much stone at any crucial place he had only two alternatives.

An honest sculptor would destroy the whole statue and start all over again. A dishonest sculptor would add something. He would take a little wax, colour it with the colour of stone, and sell it as a perfect piece of art.

Of course, with time and the changes of temperature, the flaw would appear.

So, the sculptors put out the sign "Sine cera"—without wax—to assure their customers that they could have confidence in them. Those two words are the derivation of our word "sincere"—whole, incorrupted.

To teach, not to preach. To act, not to prate. Without masks and without wax. That is how the confident life is molded and shaped, in acts and feelings that endure long after the actors have left the stage.

CHILDREN NEED GUIDANCE WITHOUT COERCION

We have succeeded in enthroning the child as king. He can do no wrong. And if, perchance, he does err, we must not chastise or discipline him—heaven forfend! Freudian hobgoblins may one day emerge in complexes which will make men intent upon killing their fathers or women sure to destroy their mothers.

The child is not only king: He is God. Some people love God, but most fear Him. So with parents. They are warned by psychiatrists that they must love their children. But they cannot overcome the fear of their children. They fear their wrath and at every turn seek to appease their anger.

The "cult of the child" has reached such proportions that in many ways our children are no longer children. They are wilful dictators, pint-sized Caesars, little Napoleons, who have become the important decision-makers of family life.

One of the proper and natural needs of childhood is to learn how to play. But we have succumbed to this demand by elevating it to an absurd height, thus making it the most important goal of child-life.

While much of our childhood should be spent in learning how to play and in acquiring habits of unburdened and unhurried happiness, parents have yielded to the "divine dicta" of their little Johnnies. With what result? We are guilty of making our children seek a lifetime of play; of preparing them for a career of continued irresponsibility.

Parents need to be the real decision-makers, the moral guides and teachers who love but do not fear their young ones, who discipline their children without violating their integrity as human beings. Tolerance is needed; but not that brand of apathy called tolerance, which supposes that people can live hopefully without convictions, loyalties, and profound commitments.

The path of least resistance does not lead to tolerance or confidence; it brings us to the state of inertia and spiritual paralysis. Tolerant, confident parents recognize that means and ends must not be confused or transposed; nor do they permit the final destination to become less important than the ways of reaching the goals of life.

On the other hand, parents must avoid going to the other extreme. They must not make childhood a time for undue responsibility and harsh duty. Delicate insight makes us realize that children will be children; they surely need relaxed leisure; they should not wilfully be denied all of the pleasure of happy and easy times.

Life consists, after all, not only of responses to duty and challenge, but also of sweet simplicities. Growing older we must still remember how to play; we must re-discover the simple, naive, and unsophisticated joys of life.

One philosopher has taught: "A clash of doctrines is not a disaster—it is an opportunity." So with the rebellions of children. Inevitably, in the process of maturation, they must rebel. They will kick over some traces of their parents, but we ought to expect that. They will yet find themselves, if they have been schooled to know what to look for.

Wise parents will not seek to exercise the authority of coercion; if they do, they will be stiffly met, challenged, and perhaps overwhelmed. Rather should they cultivate the more lasting, more ethical, and more sensible authority of influence; even then they must expect to be challenged. But then, that challenge will more likely be an opportunity, not a disaster.

The confident parent balances himself between the two extremes. He leads his children without oppressing them. He holds on to the guide-lines of life. But he doesn't pull too hard, or else, they will tear!

CHILDREN NEED
A SENSE OF DIRECTION

Someone has said that good children are those who make little trouble for their elders.

Maybe a little light can be thrown on the problem of juvenile delinquency by paraphrasing that proposition:

Good parents are those who make little trouble for their children.

We're not the first to blame the younger generation for the troubles of the time. In a museum at Istanbul there is a tablet almost 6,000 years old, on which is inscribed:

"We have fallen upon evil times and the world has waxed very old and wicked. Politics are very corrupt. Children are no longer respectful to their parents."

Children often become the convenient scapegoat for the misdeeds of their elders. But instead of blaming the "juvenile delinquents" we ought to think about delinquent parents.

Parents possess what the French call "noblesse oblige"—the obligations that come with special privileges.

For there is no greater glory or deeper beauty than the privilege of parenthood. And for this gift parents must pay the price in terms of sacrifice, of responsibility, of dedication, and of steadfastness.

When Stokowski came to Philadelphia to conduct the city's symphony orchestra, he was told that on the whole the orchestra was a good one. His advisers added:

"But only the first violins are first rate. The other sections are not. You ought to spend more time with these, to bring them up to the level of the first violins."

Whereupon Stokowski replied:

"Oh no, my friends. I shall do just the reverse. It will be my task to help make the first violins even better. As the leaders improve, to keep pace with them, the others will too."

And so with parents—the leaders of society.

Instead of bemoaning the deeds or misdeeds of children, let's find out how parents are setting the patterns of their children's behaviour.

Modern parents seem to pride themselves in the fact that they are very free with their children, that they run a very democratic home. But, too often, our children are tired of making decisions for themselves, all by themselves.

There always comes a time in the life of our children when they ask the question of the little girl in the progressive school:

"Teacher, today again must we do what we want to do?"

If parents would be parents, children could be children. As it is, both are confused because their roles are mixed. A child who really doesn't know his own mind cannot be guided by a parent who tells him:

"It is up to you. Make up your own mind."

A parent must be a teacher and as a good teacher he has to be prepared: Goals, lesson plans, good motivations—all are necessary tools of the parent. Two and two equal four, and the lesson cannot end by saying they equal five just because the children make it so.

But, of course, a good teacher believes they equal four, knows they equal four, and shows how they equal four—and the children accept it and learn it.

The difficulty with some parents, to carry the analogy further, is that they don't know what counts and therefore everything seems to add up to nothing. They believe in little, know little, transmit little. And their children are not led. They just wonder and wander.

Freedom that is not anarchy subsists on laws. And parents had better lay down some minimum ground rules for their home life.

Love is the heart of the home. But law is its flesh and muscle. Both are needed. Our children deserve our tender love. They need to feel wanted. But they richly deserve to have confidence in their parents. They need to know what it is we want for ourselves and for them.

As long as parents are too lazy or uninterested to raise their own standards of thinking and doing, we can't expect anything better of their children.

The defects of the original show up clearly in the carbon copy. Too many parents have never sought to find life's answers themselves. Instead of confidence they transmit confusion.

You've heard people sighing over what they wish their children to be.   You ought to ask them first:

"What is it that you are or intend to be?"

When parents possess the confident awareness of who they are, what they are, whence they came, and whither they are going, children are usually not problem children—because the parents are not problem parents.

CHILDREN NEED
TO LEARN TOLERANCE

There is one sin that is most difficult to dislodge.   That is so because everybody denounces it and hardly anyone confesses it.   It is the sin of prejudice.

Or if we do own up to it, we generally smile away our prejudices as something not very serious.

Prejudice begins where charity or hate or fear begins— in our homes.   It is not so much taught as it is caught from the home and from the parents who shelter us in childhood.   Someone has aptly said:

"We are tatooed with the beliefs of our tribe when we are in the cradle."

Parents have a way of blaming their proxy agents for the misdeeds or spiritual deformities of their children.   Either the schools or the clubs, the churches or the synagogues become the targets for blame.   But delinquent children are created by delinquent parents.

And so with our prejudices.   Our children soak up our hates and our peeves.   And forever after they will bruise and abuse innocent people because of parents who were thoughtless.

The trouble is that our homes no longer are the vital centre of our lives. Church attendance may be on the upgrade, but family life seems to be on the decline.

No one man may be indispensable, but for the good, good homes are.

We need a place where we foster the uniqueness of each personality, where love can take root and blossom forth.

We need a place where our rights and duties are recognized, where our differences are respected. We need a place where we can be in the minority and still survive creatively. This a good home provides.

Democratic life requires a recognition that at some point in our lives every one of us belongs to a minority. Somewhere along the line, whether it concern our religious, political, philosophical, economic, or cultural interests, every man should be able to be proud of his right to be different. And without penalty. When he has caught this attitude from his home, he will infect everyone he meets with the same spirit.

The trouble with some of us is that we are abysmally ignorant of other people as well as being ignorant of our own selves. Someone has correctly said: "To have a prejudice is to be down on something you are not up on!"

But ignorance should be no excuse.

The American poet, Robert Frost, tells of a New England farmer who was patching stone walls which cold weather had damaged. As he looked up, he said:

"Something there is that doesn't love a wall. That Something is God!"

Tend your own garden. But let your neighbour's grow as well.

CHILDREN NEED
TO "FEEL" RELIGIOUS

When your little ones ask: "Who made the world?" they may pick you up with a start. Remember, some of the most profound, thought-provoking questions are asked not by members of the learned fraternity but by three-, four-, and five-year-olds. But despite their "profundities" please remember their age. In your flushed bewilderment, guard against confusing them with a complex theology.

Religion sometimes has to be saved from the hands of its friends. Small children have little talent for making value-judgments. The adult portrait of God which we impose upon them satisfies our deepest adult needs; it often neglects the emotional needs of the children.

Strange things happen, and later, when these youngsters grow into maturity, the hobgoblins of confusion re-appear and confidence dwindles. Paradoxically, those adults who cannot keep their balance in a day of trouble, whose conception of God remains forever childish, are probably the very ones who, as children, were offered an adult God long before they ever felt such a need.

For any idea to take root and find its mark in our life and habit, we must first *feel* the need of it.

One does not become "religious" at a given moment, or at the drop of a dogma, creed, or doctrine. The religious attitude does not come about via the route of sacred vocabulary or theological platform. It arises out of personal feelings, needs, and desires.

If we begin with the child's needs, we will be quick to recognize that he understands and enjoys the tangible and the visible. The props, aids, and symbols of the various ritual traditions are just what the three- and four-year-olds need.

Ritual offers the child a picturesque, imaginative, and visible poetry which he himself can act out. He becomes the doer, the hero of the play, the subject—not the object—of religious activity.

Ritual habits are fraught with meaning to the pre-school child, because they reach him on the major level of his experience—the feeling level.

Our pre-school children do not know the meaning of reality, but they know the universalized language of feeling.

Strangely, then, a home may be filled with a lot of talk about God and really be transmitting little religion. Children have to "feel religion", not just hear about it.

Only after feeling God can they come to know Him and gain the confidence that such knowledge gives.

CHILDREN NEED A GOD THEY WILL UNDERSTAND

There are some parents who exploit God instead of explaining Him. Using God as a kind of cosmic truant officer, they deprive their children of the understanding of God that is required for confident living. These unimaginative parents fall into three groups: Those who make God into an administrative assistant, or a policeman in the sky, or a personal bodyguard.

Those for whom God functions as their administrative assistant "call upon Him" to get the child to do something they want done, but cannot get him to do. Sorry results of this kind of divine exploitation abound.

Think of all the adults who have thrown God out of their lives because He represents someone "who gets you to do things you don't want to do". Not a few of the so-called liberals of our generation who have rejected a religious code of life as fantastic are products of elders who weakly loaded their parental responsibilities upon some heavenly assistant.

Children who are told that "God wants you to do this" must first be taught why their parents want it, why such behaviour is not only expected, but beneficial.

Most of us have met parents who use God as "a policeman in the sky". This is the product of moral laziness. God is fashioned into a perennial agent of wrath. The child is constantly barraged with the threat, "God will punish you!"

Brimstone religion makes little sense to children who are seeking security and dependability. It may frighten the devil out of our children. But forever after, God seems to be the devil's sponsor; His face wears a thousand fiendish masks.

Children also are misled by the parent who fashions God into a "personal bodyguard". The child is taught to think of Him as an invisible, powerful, private overseer, who will save him from harm.

To be sure, God is known intimately as a friend and watchman, but only for those near and dear. Emotional breakdowns among adults often reveal this warped teaching in childhood.

The test of vital religion always arises when trial and tragedy enter our lives. Often, those who imagined themselves faithful believers in God, on looking at the face of death or sickness, suddenly discover that they have been robbed of their confidence in God and nothing remains of their faith.

They always have relied on God as their personal bodygaurd, and cannot understand why tragedy has come to them.

Children need to be taught about God. But their parents must help give them a conception of God which will prepare them for mature living.

Children must grow towards God, not away from Him. Spiritual growth, like physical development, never happens all at once. God is patient; He waits for children to become adults!

CHILDREN NEED
A SPIRITUAL LEGACY

What is a legacy? Is it only the counting out of spoils apportioned mathematically to those we leave behind? Or may it also be a spiritual bequest, a rule and guide for those who will live with our name long after we are gone.

Hundreds of years ago, among medieval Jews, there developed the custom of writing "ethical wills"—testaments of the spirit, which fathers left for their children.

Reproduced in the lines which follow are extracts of one such guide, written at the beginning of the fourteenth century by a well-known scholar, Rabbi Asher ben Yehiel. It still stands as a pithy reminder of what we might teach our own children, in life as well as in death.

"These are the things to which thou must give heed, if thou wouldst depart from the snares of death, and bask in the light of life!

"Be not prone to enter into quarrels; beware of oppressing fellow men, whether in money or word. Never feel envy or hate. Rely not on the broken reed of human support, make not gold thy hope, for therein lies the first step to idolatry. 'Tis a fine and right course to think little of thy virtues and much of thy vices; to magnify the mercies of Him who made thee and provideth thy sustenance in due season. Act not aright from hope of reward, nor avoid the wrong from fear of punishment; but serve from love. Esteem the utterance of thy money as of less import than the utterance of thy words. . . . Hide behind the walls of thy heart what is said in thy presence, even though thou be not pledged to confidence. If thou hearest the same report from another, say not: 'I have heard it already!'

" . . . Speak not insolence with a haughty neck, lifting high thy forehead, thereby rejecting the fear of heaven. Never do in private what thou wouldst be ashamed to do in public, and say not: 'Who will see me?' . . .

" . . . Raise not thine hand against thy neighbour. Circulate no false reports; slander no man. Put not thy fellow man to the blush in public. Never be weary of making friends, consider a single enemy as one too many. If thou hast a faithful friend, hold fast to him; let him not go, for he is a precious possession. But entice not friendship by adulation and hypocrisy, and speak not with a double heart! Retain not thine anger against a fellow man for a single day, but humble thyself and ask forgiveness. Let not thy heart be high, saying: I am the injured party, let him make the first overtures! But every night before thou retirest to rest, forgive whoever has offended thee . . .

" . . . Never utter a falsehood, but be faithful to all men, irrespective of creed. Be not slow to offer the greeting of peace to all, be they Jew or Gentile; and never give a fellow man cause for resentment . . .

" . . . Show invariable hospitality to wayfarers; welcome them with a smiling face . . .

" . . . Never be angry with thy wife; if thou put her off from thee with thy left hand, delay not to draw her to thee again with thy right hand! . . .

" . . . Be ever responsive to the call of charity! . . . "

Part VI

KNOW THE WONDER
OF CONFIDENCE
IN GOD

FAITH KEEPS YOU
FROM FALSE WORSHIP

We are anxious, perhaps, because we are worshipping gods who mock us. We have made a religion of success. Too many think that in order to be happy we must pursue success and that the man who does not do so must be unhappy indeed. But the pursuit of success makes a man too anxious to be really happy.

In the "religion of success", money has become the accepted measure of "salvation". A man who makes a lot of money is a clever fellow; a man who does not, is not. And nobody likes to be thought a fool; and an unsuccessful fool, at that. And unsuccessful fools can only live in fools' paradise.

The religion of success breeds still another false and vain pursuit—the cult of "peace of mind". Some think that this is the key to personal happiness. But this search turns out to be a detour, because it leads us away from reality.

No force on earth can help a man until he faces up to himself and recovers his sense of reality. Some things there are in life which we just cannot have. We end up in morbid despair trying to have what cannot be had, instead of learning how to live with what we've got.

Here is a woman destroying her life because of prolonged bereavement, not knowing what to make of her trouble. And there is a man who lives in unholy misery because all he can see is his neighbour's success. He hasn't the eyes to see what he himself possesses.

Much of our cynicism is the result of our wrong worship, our mixed-up values. We make ourselves the centre of the universe, and seek to mold the world to our own vanities and comforts.

Gandhi's worldly possessions were photographed after his death, and anyone who has seen this remarkable picture must be moved to a sharper understanding of the meaning of life.

This great world leader left only these physical possessions: two pairs of sandals, two eating bowls, a pair of spectacles, a spoon, a knife, a fork, and a book of Hindu Scripture. But he left a spiritual legacy that is the common property of a large part of civilized humanity.

The first great lesson taught by Gandhi was that unless you are free in your own mind, no man can free you. Not even Moses could free the Israelites as long as they were not free men in their own eyes. Before emancipation there must first come auto-emancipation.

Gandhi taught something else. Loyal to his own tradition, profoundly attached to the Hindu religion, he saw the whole world before him. How can you achieve this broad perspective? Gandhi was able to do it because of his penetrating religious thought. In essence he said that the only way to resolve a conflict between what I hold to be dear and what is dear to other men is to see all of us as subjected to the will of the same God.

When we understand the unity of God, we may come to appreciate the unity of mankind.

FAITH SAYS:
KNOW GOD BY WHAT HE DOES!

I once heard a lesson a mother gave her inquiring six-year-old. The child asked her what God was like. And the mother answered by taking two glasses of water and setting them down on the kitchen table.

"Darling," she said, "taste from this glass", and she pointed to the first. The child drank. "Now take some of this granulated sugar, put it into the second glass, and stir it well."

The child did it. "Now drink the water", the mother suggested. "And tell me, how does it taste?" The child told the mother of the sweet, sweet taste of the water.

"Can you see the sugar?"

"No, Mother. But I can taste it."

"Darling, that is just the way God works in His world. We never see Him. But because we know that there are sweet and kind and good people in the world, even though we cannot see God, we know that He makes things that way. Just like sugar in the glass of water."

In every simple but beautiful explanation of basic qualities of life, there is a profound depth that lies under the surface. This mother was speaking of God in the language of a six-year-old. But in a sense she penetrated into the deepest reaches of man's soul.

Very often we use words as a substitute or a camouflage for our lack of real feeling. But you cannot truly understand something until you have also felt it. And the mere mouthing of high-sounding syllables is not enough. It is sometimes rather deluding.

Strangely enough, the things we come to know through our personal feelings turn out to be the simplest to explain. That is because we are not relying only on the thoughts and descriptions of others. We have got something important to say when our words grow out of our own inner experiences.

This mother was probably able to explain God to her child in this profoundly simple way because she confidently felt that way herself.

The Psalmist said: "Taste and you shall see that the Lord is good." This mother had herself tasted and knew what to give her child.

God is more than a concept to be discussed, debated, or analyzed. God is known not so much by what He is, as by what He does. Only when God is personally experienced, can faith produce confidence.

FAITH URGES:
FIND GOD DESPITE YOUR DOUBTS!

How do you find God in a difficult time? The century in which we live is one in which it has not been easy to believe in God. Suffering and the threat of war have shaken our religious convictions to their foundations. The question on many people's lips is: Where is God now?

Even the believing man is often plagued with great doubts. But doubt, paradoxically, has always accompanied man in his quest after God. Abraham, God's first messenger, also doubted. He, too, wondered where God was and in seeking the salvation of Sodom and Gomorrah longed for the mercy of God. The Psalmist spoke of those who tormented him with the taunt: "Where now is thy God?" And the prophet

Habakkuk testifies eloquently that even among religious people God is often lost from view, His power mocked. "O Lord, how long shall I cry and Thou wilt not hear? Even when I cry out unto Thee out of violence Thou wilt not save. Why dost Thou show me iniquity and cause me to behold grievance?"

We ask: Where is God? Perhaps we had better begin with ourselves, asking: Where are we? God is in the moral law of the universe which calls upon us to stop retreating from responsibility and to begin upholding the law. But where are we? We say that God has failed us; that we are still waiting for Him to change the world. Have we ever considered that perhaps we have failed Him by ignoring His law? Perhaps it is God who waits patiently for us.

The mortal suffering we produce and the inter-human tension we create are perhaps the best proof available that God is working in the world! If we could go on selfishly keeping and enjoying our advantage, while the rest of the world lacks, this then would truly be a mad world. If we could go on hating people because of skin colour, creed, wealth, or talent, and still enjoy harmony and peace, this, then, would be an immoral universe.

Doubt, then, helps those who are on the edge of despair find meaning in the midst of grave and serious confusions. It is one of the great and strange circumstances of life and history that in periods of doubts, question, and search, God has been found by many.

In self-satisfied, easy-going, prosperous communities, God is hardly ever found, for He is never needed. In times of trouble it may appear there is no God; and yet history indicates that it is only in times of trouble that man finds God. Only when man thinks seriously about himself and the world, when he has been thrown into the depths and tries to struggle out of his despair, can he find God.

It is perhaps such a thought which prompted a well-known writer to say: "If you want safe religion with all doubts removed you can easily find it—if you promise not to think. But if you want a live religion—you will have to go fishing in your own soul and catch it."

Albert Camus, French novelist and Nobel Prize winner, has artfully described the condition of modern man in a fable revealing Sisyphus, the Greek who was condemned by the gods and punished. Modern man, says Camus, is symbolized in the punishment meted out to Sisyphus. And what was his punishment? Sisyphus was condemned to rolling stones up the side of a mountain, and given the charge to bring them to the top. But once he reached the top, he was required to roll them down again—to begin again his fruitless, enervating labour. He is sentenced to countless, futile curcuits.

This, indeed, is the situation of modern man: He labours and toils in a dreary round. He thinks he can reach the top. But the top is only a snare and a delusion, for no sooner does he get to the peak, when he must begin all over again. This is a Greek view of man's tragedy, and perhaps such a morbid fatalism is the reason for the rampant materialism of our day.

The Greeks suggested what seemed to them the most practical answer—an answer which might be summed up in the cry of many men without faith: Eat, drink, and be merry, for tomorrow we die! If there is no peak to which one may aspire, if all life is indeed a wasteful running in circles, then why should we not follow the Greek hedonist?

But the story of Moses and the history of his faith teach another lesson. Moses knew that he himself would never get to the Promised Land; he would die before setting foot upon it. But the religious view departs from the Greek view: It continues to believe in the hope that man can ultimately find freedom and emancipation.

Moses had to experience, personally, the evils of Egypt, feel the lash of the taskmaster's tongue and whip, before he could long for a promised land. Only when a man personally feels the evils of an Egypt can he dream of a land of hope.

Humans are strange creatures. We either refuse or are unable to learn from the experience of others. In one philosopher's words: "History teaches that history teaches nothing."

One man knew that truth poignantly when he confessed: "I have made much money in life. I have amassed a great fortune. You would think that I should be happy. But I am not! My greatest sorrow is that while I can offer my children wealth and fortune, I cannot give them my experience. There is nothing that I can do to prevent sorrow. They will have to experience these for themselves."

Perhaps this explains why evil is in the world: To help smug goodness take stock of itself! God hardened Pharaoh's heart. Had He not, perhaps the Israelites would have remained in Egypt. Evil becomes so evil that good people must ultimately shatter their own doubts, move away from easy complacency and strike forth boldly to glimpse a better world.

Despite the fact that some men die, that some men are doomed to destruction, mankind is not doomed, the future is never without hope! Why? Because the faithful attitude towards life has confidence that this is a moral universe in spite of immorality; it stakes its commitment on the hope that Pharaohs can be destroyed; their "victory" is only temporary victory. If we resign ourselves to a belief that Pharaoh will triumph over us, then we consign our future to the grimness of the present; we shall remain in a thousand Egypts through all of the time to come.

Where is God? In the midst of our doubts He is waiting for our faith. Starting with doubt, we achieve confidence if we keep the land of promise in view.

FAITH PROCLAIMS:
BELIEVING IS SEEING!

You discuss a problem with your friend and he nods and says: "I see what you mean."

Or you encourage another to reach out for some worthy achievement by telling him to "rise to the occasion."

And when doubt gnaws at your inners, you try to overcome it by exhorting yourself to "stand up to life."

In none of these situations has anyone actually "seen", or "risen", or "stood up".

We're always having problems with language. Words cannot easily communicate deeply felt emotions. That's because we never can see, hear, touch, taste, or smell a powerful insight or a strong sentiment. And yet, we must use language to convey our certainty and our conviction about our deepest feelings. But it has its risks.

That is why there is so much misunderstanding abroad about what faith means in our lives. Man can only feebly describe to others his deepest feelings.

The language of faith is not the language of words. It is expressed in moods, in attitudes, in moments that transcend doubt and despair. It is the feeling of gratitude for the life of each day.

When we strait-jacket faith into words, we're apt to be more concerned with what it sounds like and forget what it feels like. Or when we compress faith into images, we are apt to concentrate upon what it looks like.

Sixty-three years before the Christian era, Pompey set out to find the secret of the people of Palestine. He stormed Jerusalem; obsessed by a single passion, he made his way past the guards of Mount Zion.   He would enter the Holy of Holies to see and hear for himself the mystery of the unusual religion of that land.

And there he found—we all know what—nothing but an empty room!

Consider this perplexity of this leader of the West, standing in the presence of a sacred emptiness. He who believed that only physical might could make a people strong and give it stature, that only empires and armies availed, looked into the unseen face of a mystery that still evaded him.

The mystery of the "empty room" evades us still.   To some it seems senseless because it goes beyond the report of our sight, sound, touch, smell, or taste.

But we come to our senses only when we try to penetrate the potency of this force.

It is the power we get when we have reverence for life.   It is the recognition of the sacred dimensions of human striving, the courage to believe in the triumph of righteousness in the teeth of evil.

It is the feeling of being in tune with the eternal rhythm of the universe, the surge of strength that comes when God is magnified because human life is sanctified.

We tend to think of religion as something that goes on only inside churches and synagogues, instead of knowing for ourselves the vital, surging power we have within us.

There are those who look upon faith as unreal until proven valid in the test tubes of scientific experiment.   Faith, like a purple cow, can't be real, they would say.   Have you ever seen it?

The man of faith doesn't need to argue.   He confidently knows that seeing isn't believing.   Believing is seeing.

FAITH GIVES PURPOSE TO LIFE

"In the beginning God . . ."

Genesis is not a book of science; it is a book of wisdom. The author does not describe the scientific process of creation. He is not concerned with these things. He is concerned with the fact of creation; he proclaims without embarrassment that the world did not spring into being chaotically or accidentally, without plan, design, or purpose.

"In the beginning God . . ."

For the spiritual man all of life flows from this resounding, joyful, and exciting affirmation. Given God, the world with all of its sorrow, travail, and pain may still have meaning. Without God, nothing is truly significant; even our victories, triumphs, and glories are empty and hollow.

You cannot prove creation in the test-tubes of a laboratory. Indeed, no scientist worthy of the name would admit that it is possible to disprove it. Strange as it may seem, the profound man of science is the most potential believer in creation.

No scientist ever "saw" an electron; nor does he think that anyone ever could. Yet, nothing is more "real" to a scientist than an electron.

Most of us would call a table or a chair real because we can see or touch them. But a scientist knows that the table and the chair are not real, even though they can be seen or touched.

The table and the chair, to a scientist, are nothing more than a swirling set of electric charges which he calls electrons.

The author of Genesis is concerned—vitally concerned—with the answer to the question of what man is. He is not specific regarding how man developed from the lower species. Silence reigns on that issue; for the author is not a scientist. Genesis says only that man was created at the top of the scale, after all other species had been formed.

But what is said? "God made man out of the dust of the earth." Here, in the language of symbolism, are imbedded two ideas—not facts—that matter supremely. Man is nothing; he is like dust.

Physically, he declines, erodes, and decays; for he is eminently finite. But man was formed as the crown and the pinnacle of all creation.

The biologist asks: What is man? And he answers: "He is but one step removed from his cousins of the animal kingdom"

To which, the man of spirit, basing his life upon the intimations of Genesis, can reply: Man may be these things; yet, please remember: Man is also the biologist. He is a mere creature; but because he has been created to strive and to search, to rule and to serve, a divine spark animates him. Physically, he is nothing; spiritually, he can be something.

And what is most important: When we have the confidence that spiritually we can become something, that there is plan and purpose to life, we no longer remain animals but become men.

FAITH DEMANDS
REVERENCE FOR LIFE

There can be no science without doubt, nor any religion without a keen, sharp sense of wonder.

There is a kind of knowledge, gained by methods we call scientific, which can never be acquired without a hesitancy to accept facts without challenge, investigation, and denial.

But knowing something is not the same as understanding it. Analysis of an idea does not necessarily give us a penetrating insight. A literary critic may dissect a poem, but only a poet can create it.

That is why a photograph of a scene is not the same as the artist's painting of it. To be sure, the former attempts to be objective while the latter can only be personal and subjective.

But all insights are drawn from the inner world of man's thought. They are not the careful results of probes and gauges, of tests or measurements.

An artist, therefore, makes no claims of knowing anything. But he tries to understand everything. And he does this by a method that is a scandal to the scientific mind. He does this through an intimate inter-action with the world that surrounds him.

He does this by being a participant and not a detached observer. If he were only eyes, he would be a camera, or if only mind, a computation machine.

But he has a sense of what is good or evil, beautiful or ugly, tragic or comic, grand or paltry. He is anything but objective. But as long as he is concerned with values and not statistics he never can completely divorce his own self from what he sees. The moment he loses his personal sense of wonder, of amazement and awe, he destroys his art and forfeits his mission.

Many of us are dogged, hard workers, pursuing tasks with zeal and devotion. That is important. But only technically important. Many books are technically good. They are flawlessly written, carefully planned. But they lack the spark, the flash of insight. On the surface they are neatly arranged. But they never reach beneath the surface.

There are musicians and painters who may be master crafts-men. But again only in a technical sense. An inspired artist can move you to tears or to laughter. He can raise your hopes or make you feel the pain, misery, joy, and gladness of life. He can do this only because he has felt, known, and understood these things in an intimate flash of insight which goes by the name of inspiration. Perspiration alone won't do these things.

An inspired person is one who has drawn within himself the breath of life. A confident spirit moves him. He has a vision, a horizon he's trying to touch and reach. He can move you beyond yourself, to be more than yourself.

A technician, on the other hand, is too much head and not enough heart. He may know all the rules and tools of his trade and yet never get to the heart of the matter.

This is why inspired parents are not the products of courses in child psychology alone. Besides knowing something about the method of child-raising, a hopeful, buoyant spirit must sing within itself about the deepest purposes of life.

Nor are teachers created by other teachers alone. Method is much, but not all. For even the unimaginative can hide a lack of insight behind the cloak of technical efficiency. Indeed, there is madness in a method that doesn't go beyond method.

A scientist who lacks moral convictions may think himself a better scientist for it. He may end up less a man, however. For scientific skill is only a method, a means, not an end.

Religion is the art of life; from faith in God there comes a determination to live with confidence and trust in the tremendous majesty and goodness of His world. It has no argument with science as long as science reports what it knows.

But it suggests that beyond knowledge there is feeling, and out of feeling there comes understanding, and sometimes even wisdom.

And it is wisdom we need more than knowledge. Knowledge is the accumulation of facts. Wisdom tells us how to evaluate them.

All of us know educated boors who went to a string of colleges but never learned how to live.

Universities have been turning out men who know everything about trifles and a trifle about everything. It is often a case of too little and too much. College graduates know too much about too little and too little about too much.

Perhaps that is why education, by itself, cannot save the world. Not if by education we mean the acquisition of facts which may be proved quite true, but which do not make the slightest dent upon the way we live with ourselves and with others.

One religious teacher said: The prayer that doesn't inspire the deed is impious.

So with our education. If our minds become merely a deep freeze for the cold storage of facts once learned, then we might as well be done with the search for light and begin looking for some heat. And heat is generated by an inner spark of character that glows even when the mind may be in the dark.

It is not so much what a man knows that counts but how he uses what he knows.

Knowledge is power but the beginning of wisdom is reverence.

We have unlocked the secret doors of nature and opened them to our minds. But with all of our knowledge we are still afraid of each other, because we don't know what we may do with our strength.

We need to inculcate reverence for life before we can diminish our fear of death. To do this we must reach below the neck. Besides good minds we need big hearts. We need hearts that are firmly rooted in a confident faith in a religious way of life.

At home, in the school, and in the world around us we are in danger of self-destruction. We have so much technical "know-how" without enough moral "know-why". Knowledge that is imparted without an inspired passion for its righteous use may yet tyrannize us all.

From sheer skill we need to grow to the moral ends, from method to motivation, from mere craftsmanship to real art. And the ultimate art is religion.

FAITH CREATES
RESPECT FOR MORALITY

All of us—not just the scientists—need to know of nature's laws; but nature's laws, we ought to remember, are not invented by the scientist. They are discovered by him. But once he discovers them, or better still, once they are revealed to him, he teaches us to respect them. And respect is based upon normal common sense.

No man in his right mind would wittingly tempt fate by breaking a law of nature.

Noble and peasant, the arrogant and humble alike are subject to its consequences. Times and circumstances, creeds or colours cannot and do not alter or abolish it.

Take the law of gravity. Whether you live in Asia or America, when you fall you can only fall down—not up.

Once a Hebrew prophet told his people: You know there is no escape from the law of nature. Know, too, that you cannot retreat from the laws of morality. Both were promulgated by the One Creator.

It was Amos who said:

"Will a lion roar in the forest when he hath no prey?

"Will a bird fall in a snare upon the earth when there is no lure for it?

"Shall evil befall a city and the Lord hath not done it?"

Our trouble is this: We respect the laws of nature because we can see their immediate consequences. We overlook the laws of ethics because we think we can "get away with it".

Well, we've gotten away with nothing. Every cause has its effect. We pay a heavy price for everything we "get away with".

Perhaps if we respected the Author of the law as much as its human discoverers, we'd live better, long, and happier.

A conversation between two men—one a wise, elderly sage, the other a young and unseasoned student—sheds clear light on the question at hand. The older man, out of his bitter experience, was suggesting that morality was the basis of all human hope and confidence.

He had just come from Europe. The war was over. He had seen many buildings shattered, big and small ones. The ruins of blitzed cities came to his eyes as he looked up to view the heights of New York's tall buildings.

And then he spoke to his young friend.

"What makes these buildings stand so tall, so firm? Can you tell me?"

And he went on without waiting for an answer.

"Yes, I know of Pittsburgh, its iron and its steel. And I know, too, of your quarries, your stone and granite. You have a treasure house of nature, and from it you have put together great cities by the genius of man's mind.

"But we in Europe have some of these things, too. We have steel and iron and granite. And our buildings have fallen.

"Do you know what keeps your buildings from falling and why ours are dashed to the ground?"

Once again he continued without hesitation.

"I will tell you. No buildings stand anywhere in the world because of the strength of their materials or the craftsmanship of their designers. Homes and schools, factories and farms, office buildings and skyscrapers have a foundation which is invisible. They are based upon the moral law.

"When you destroy the moral law, as we did, you have destroyed the building, because you have removed its very foundation."

And the young friend looked up at the tall skyscraper. He scanned it with his eyes quickly, from top to bottom. He could not "see" what the wise old man meant. But he understood.

FAITH MAKES FOR SELF-RESPECT

There is nothing as permanent in the world as change.

The twentieth century is no different in that respect from the eras that preceded us, with one exception: the rapidity of the changes.

It used to take generations before anything new could penetrate human living. Now, inventions and discoveries occur with such quickening pace that the face of the earth changes often within a single lifetime.

But the naked eye sees only the obvious changes of travel and communication—radio, television, jet planes, and the telephone. The more important changes we can't see as easily.

These are the changes in our values, the changes in our attitudes and points of view, in what we make important or deem unimportant.

What was once dear and precious is now considered trivial or, at best, optional. What was once cheap and perhaps even vulgar is now thought to be important and worthwhile.

We have moved, in our time, from morals to morale. We have no special code of conduct of our own. We just want to keep up our acceptance on the part of others—just keep up the morale!

The result is that we develop standards which are no standards, which change with the passing fancy and the passing fad.

Our new God is "self-expression". But what are we expressing? The finest, the noblest, the best that is in us? Or is self-expression for many an excuse for vulgarity, greed, and lust?

We are in peril of being reduced to mediocrity. We like what everybody likes and dislike what everybody else dislikes. We go where everybody else goes and say what everybody says. We are even dangerously close to thinking what everyone else is thinking.

To be redeemed from mediocrity, we need to stand aside from the crowd, to know what we stand for, and what we won't stand for.

We need to develop codes of our own that reflect our deepest and our finest. We need the moral courage to protest and to dissent from the majority when the majority has succumbed to error and vulgarity.

Often, we protest too much against others as a cover-up for our own failures. This is a false kind of protest which turns out to be a misuse of a wonderful instrument.

What is the right protest?

President Woodrow Wilson said that no matter how busy he was, he was always willing to find time to see Rabbi Stephen Wise, whenever the latter called for an appointment. Too many people, the President explained, would come to him to criticize or to offer suggestions, to protest or to dissent in the name of a cause which turned out to be nothing less than self-promotion.

Dr. Wise, the President said, never came to ask for anything for himself; he dealt only with the moral issues and with the principles involved.

Yes, we need to learn self-expression. But first, we must ask the deeper question: What kind of a self are we really expressing?

True self-expression is based upon the recognition that we are humans and not animals; we are moral creatures subject to the laws of morality.

When we lack faith in the moral quality of man's personality, we ultimately lose control of our real selves. This is the deepest reason for the lack of self-confidence: We have lost the first requirement for self-respect. More than an emotional failure, the lack of self-confidence is a sign of moral weakness.

FAITH EXCLAIMS:
LIVE PRAYERFULLY!

A lot of people are confused about the meaning of prayer. Some people consider it merely as a supplication or petition, or what someone has called "lobbying in the halls of the Divine".

True, some prayer is like that. Some prayer reflects "fox-hole religion"—the shriek of fright in the midst of emergency and crisis. But let us not be so intellectually snobbish that we urge these needs out of human life. One might as well say never cry; it is non-rational to cry. Yet, just as man is made to laugh, he is also made to cry; and there have been many tears through which we have learned to smile.

But more important is the power that comes to the human heart when we learn how to pray, not only in moments of crisis, but also in the hour of triumph.

The high purpose of real prayer may be summed up in this phrase: to evoke the best in us to meet the worst about us.

This kind of an attitude reminds us that it is impossible to expect prayers to be effective or self-realizing at once. The prayer which looks for immediate results is really not prayer, it is magic.

Why does man pray? He seeks strength and understanding to gain victory in conflict.

Essentially, there are three forms of conflict, each different in character. There is the conflict of man with nature. The human being is a frail match for powerful physical forces at work in the universe. He must seek to obey the laws he discovers, humbly to submit to those forces he cannot control. Elementary wisdom dictates that he surrender his will before a law and a force mightier than he. But much remains for him to do. He continues to wage unceasing and successful battle, triumphing over the perils of nature, by tunnelling mountains, bridging waters, and climbing to the moon.

There is, moreover, the conflict of man with man—perennially and universally. In every age and place, men have not only rubbed shoulders; they have also locked horns. They unite, but soon use their joined strength to destroy other bands of brothers. Yet, the recognition of civil wars' folly sometimes leads men to an equivalent understanding that fratricide leads to suicide. Though no good, sane man would say that wars are good in themselves, history shows that wars have sometimes led to thoughts of peace.

The principal conflict facing man is, of course, his conflict with himself. As long as he remains incapable of resolving this difficulty, he will stand helpless before nature and fearful before his neighbour.

Unceasing battles go on within the inner folds of man's mind and soul. The problems of atomic energy, of international diplomacy are real and significant. But until we conquer our baser impulses and gain confidence from the power of our spirit, no other victory is truly meaningful.   Noah in the play *Green Pastures* said: "I ain't much, but I'se all I got."   We may not be very much, in contrast to nature's grandeur and to the imposing significance of the great world.   Remember though: "We're all we got!"

Real prayer induces within us an abundant, expectant, and hopeful attitude about life.   Yet, it is always tinged with the recognition of our own frailty and of a world much broader and bigger than the little orbit of our own special concerns.

The prayer which seeks immediate perfection from the hand of the Divine and which demands sudden and swift response to personal requirements, misses the vital and majestic quality of high religion.

Moses never did get to the Promised Land.   He died at the mountain top viewing his dream from afar.   But he was no failure; he was a significant spiritual success.

More of us need to remember these things.   We cannot achieve everything that we set out to achieve.   But we can move closer to the lands of our own promise.   And when we do not run from the challenge, we make it possible for our children to come still closer to its fulfillment.

Someone has said that prayer is not unlike a case presented in a Supreme Court.   The Supreme Court does not pass on hypothetical matters; it deals only with the real issues placed before it.

So with prayer.   We cannot pray for peace hypothetically, or vaguely.   We cannot pray for the abolition of poverty in some hazy, vapid way without relating ourselves personally to the poor whom we know.   If it is world peace we want, then we must search for it, not only in the abstract, but in the concrete ways in which we pursue it in our own little worlds.

Prayer, then, must primarily be thought of as an aid in becoming ourselves by overcoming ourselves.   Too often we pray for the unnecessary, irrelevant victory: over others, instead of over ourselves. Prayer must begin with ourselves as a search for our soul, as a quest for our own inner harmony, and as a reverent response to the wonder of life.

Here is the sum of it: He who does not live prayerfully cannot pray vitally. For prayer is not a manner of speech; it is a way of confident life.

88¢